LETTING GO OF THE CAMERA

Photography & the Creative Process
A Series by LensWork Publishing

On Being a Photographer
David Hurn/Magnum
and Bill Jay

The Best of EndNotes
(LensWork #83)
Bill Jay

Letting Go of the Camera
Brooks Jensen

Single Exposures
Brooks Jensen

Single Exposures 2
Brooks Jensen

To be released in 2010

Finding an Audience for Your Art
Brooks Jensen

Single Exposures 3
Brooks Jensen

LETTING GO
of the
CAMERA

*Essays on Photography
and the Creative Life*

Brooks Jensen
Editor of *LensWork*

LensWork Publishing
2004

First Edition, Third Printing October 2009

ISBN #1-888803-26-6

Published by:
LensWork Publishing, 909 Third Street, Anacortes, WA, 98221-1502 USA

www.lenswork.com

To order quantities at discount pricing, please call 1-800-659-2130

For Maureen,
refuge for every storm

CONTENTS

PREFACE

These essays were written over the course of 10 years. Now, a photographer cannot possibly make images over such a long decade without learning things in the tenth year that contradict strong beliefs from the first year. At least one hopes so. Photography changes, photographers change, and certainly the expectations of the photographer's audience change. Nonetheless, the basic ideas in these essays still ring true for me and, I surmise from those who have pestered me to gather them into book form, for those who first encountered them in the pages of *LensWork*.

It is significant that the lens is a round thing because it teaches us by its very shape that circling back is the essence of photography. In preparing these essays for publication in this book, I circled around each again, editing where new insights have been discovered through experience, rewriting where old ideas were, well, old, and touching up those passages that now seemed to have been written by a much younger photographer than I am. I will be as interested as anyone to see what edits I make 10 years from now, assuming that 10 years from now I have not been, as Ansel Adams called it, immersed in the final wash.

Artmaking is, by definition and practice, a personal thing – a most personal thing. Every artist walks their own path, learns their own way, fails and succeeds in their own time. My process is as personal, and therefore as *non sequitur* to others, as anyone's. It is, however, interesting how parallel we all travel if we take the time to look left and right. I started writing these essays for a local photo group and a few friends. They encouraged me to write more because – to my surprise – it seemed that my struggles to walk the creative path were familiar to others, my questions were their questions, my discoveries – and occasionally my answers – were useful to them. This is an embarrassing position to be in.

I can't nor do I pretend to have all (or even many) of the answers to the questions of Art or Artmaking. I can, however, hope that what I've learned and shared here might be useful to you in your process. To the extent that my ideas are helpful, I am grateful. To the extent that they are not, I recommend you discard them with all due expediency. I have far more faith in the journey ahead than the path long behind. As Basho said, "Seek not the wise men of old; seek what they sought."

Brooks Jensen
Anacortes, WA
September 2004

One

WHAT IT MEANS
TO BE AN ARTIST

As an artist and the publisher of *LensWork*, I am occasionally asked the most baffling question. Someone, usually a younger person, expresses their enthusiasm for photographic art. They tell me about a few pieces of artwork that have "blown them away" and explain that they feel as though, in photography, they have found something they have searched for all their life. (I assume by this that I am supposed to be impressed by what an inconceivable long period that is when you are a 16-, 18- or 22-year-old.) They continue, explaining that they have a vision and that Art needs them and they need Art – they are called and they must respond.

I resist the temptation to roll on the floor with laughter. Instead, I smile and ask them to continue. They tell me they have been studying the great masters of photography – like Nan Goldin and Herb Ritts – and after careful consideration they have decided to dedicate themselves to a career as a *photographic artist*. The problem is that they don't quite know what that *is*. So, they ask me, "I want to be a photographic artist. What should I do?"

I am always a bit nonplused with this question but I have, over the years, developed a bit of advice for these paragons of naiveté. Here, presented for the first time on paper, are the things you should know before throwing your life away on an art career.

1. If you are lucky, when you announce to some mentor that you are going to dedicate your life to photography, he or she will clunk you on the head with their tripod in the hope that it may knock some sense into you. Do not complain about the pain. Do not, and I repeat, do not sue them. The whack is based in compassion and in the hope that you may wake up from your delusion and pursue another course, like accounting.

2. It will take five or so precious years of your youth to earn a Master of Fine Arts degree in photography. After spending an unconscionable amount of money, time and effort to attain this degree, it will be virtually useless – at least as far as making a living with your artwork. The artwork you will be trained to create will be universally rejected, criticized for being piffle, nonsalable, non-communicative, and even laughable. It will mean a great deal to you as a personal expression but you can't buy your own artwork.

3. Do not think I am making a value statement only about the work that MFA graduates produce. You will not sell any work, regardless of the type of work you produce – *avant garde*, classic landscapes, gum bichromate, Polaroid transfers, or "calendar shots." Do you see the point? YOU WILL NEVER, EVER, EVER SELL A PIECE OF PHOTOGRAPHIC ARTWORK FOR ANY PRICE, TO ANYONE, AT ANY TIME. If you start with this premise, you will be close to correct, not be disappointed, not have any unreasonable expectations, not fantasize about unrealistic business plans, not waste money on business cards or brochures, and be gratefully delighted for every piece of art you do sell, if any.

4. Because you will not ever be able to make a living creating artwork, you will be forced to find gainful employment elsewhere. You will first decide to become a teacher of photography because that will, at least, keep you involved in the fine art photographic field. Unfortunately the 900

other MFA graduates in your graduating year will also be vying for the same four open teaching positions. This says nothing about the 896 unemployed graduates from last year, the year before, the year before that, ad infinitum.

5. Because you can neither make a living producing art-work nor teaching others to produce artwork, you will take a civilian job. You will become an auto mechanic, an accountant, a doctor, or a dentist. Other fields that will be open to you will be retail, banking, transportation, eternal grant writing, and welfare.

6. The implications of your mandatory career choice are pro-found. You will spend no less than 40 hours a week doing something you dread in order that you may have your evenings, weekends, and few pitiful weeks of vacation each year in order to create your artwork and have meaning and purpose in your life. You will therefore have no time for your family, your spouse, your children. You will have no idea what your fellow co-worker are discussing as they chat about last night's hot TV drama. Your check-book will go unreconciled for years. Your most important cooking utensil will be the microwave.

7. You will have no friends whatsoever except the people who work at the local camera store and most of the tele-phone operators at Light Impressions. They, of course, will recognize your voice and call you by your first name before you have announced who you are. They will know your credit card numbers by heart. They will *never* ask you how your project is coming along.

8. You will quickly discover how resistant materials are to becoming what you envision. Every time you click the shutter, you will create an image in your mind's eye. The film will not measure up to your expecta-tions. The print drifts even farther from your vision. When toned, matted, signed and hung on the wall, the image will look not at all like your intentions. You will then understand the true tongue-in-cheek, inside

joke in all that talk about "pre-visualization." You will not laugh. What you thought was going to be a gorgeous desert panorama will somehow have self-transformed into a contrasty abstract, looking for all the world just like that stuff growing in the bottom of your bathroom tub.

9. Frustrated by these results, you will spend no less than 15 years of your life developing your craft. You may anticipate spending about $8,000 for film, chemistry and paper in order to complete your Zone System calibrations. According to a recent survey of photographic artists, you will spend on average 4,316 hours perfecting your spot toning techniques. You will eventually give up trying to cut the perfect oval mat board and have what can be characterized as "an emotional response" – but that part of the story is so ugly I will refrain from further elaboration.

10. At your forty-seventh workshop in John Sexton's darkroom, you will hear that Ansel Adams once said, "It's the zone system, stupid, not the pinpoint system." After hearing this wisdom you will have a Zen-like enlightenment experience and immediately sell your Zone VI-modified light meter at a great financial loss.

11. Gallery owners will leave you interminably on hold while they prefer to have in-depth conversations with their plumber. You will eventually catch a gallery owner unoccupied and they will speak with you enthusiastically right up to the point where you say, "I have a portfolio I'd like to …" Click. End of conversation.

12. With enough patience and perseverance, you may actually, someday, get an appointment with a gallery owner who will tell you that your work is no good, that he has seen better work from first year students, that no one buys that kind of work any more (although it used to be hot just a few years ago), and then ask you if you have anything in a genre of work you detest.

13. You will return to that same gallery owner a year later with a portfolio of the work you have created in the

asked-for genre, after having hated producing it for the last 12 months but convincing yourself that it was justifiable because it was necessary to break into the gallery scene. You will then be told by the gallery owner that that genre is now considered passé.

14. Having discovered these truths about the art world, you will admit that the only photographs that ever sell are family portraits and commercial advertising work. You will be seriously tempted, at least for a few weeks, to become a commercial and/or portrait photographer. DO NOT SUCCUMB TO THE TEMPTATION. If you do, you will never produce another piece of artwork again. The simple truth is that after spending eight, 10 or 12 hours photographing commercially, the last thing in the world you will want to do in your evenings and weekends pick up a camera.

15. During your lifetime you can expect to lose all of your photographic equipment to burglars 2.7 times, on average. The good news is that the insurance company will give you full new value on all of your equipment just before they cancel your insurance policy. In the short term, you will gain because you will find you can replace your old gear with someone else's stolen gear and pocket the difference between the used price and the new price. This will be the most money you will have ever made as a photographer.

16. As Ted Orland has pointed out so accurately in his *Photographic Truths* poster, you will be routinely asked by your friends to photograph their weddings. Early in your career you should agree to do so, one time. Show up with your 4x5 camera, clunky wooden tripod and plenty of sheet film holders. Shoot several Polaroid tests and then ask the entire wedding party to hold still for a 45 second exposure at f/64. Explain to them that one of the advantages to working with large format cameras is that you don't have work with cumbersome lights. If this does

not suffice and they still look fidgety, explain to them the concept of reciprocity failure. You may then attend all future weddings as a mere observer.

17. There will eventually come a time when your spouse will announce that he or she would like to accompany you on one of your photographic outings. Do as you always do and arise at 4:00am to catch the early angular light. Spend all day in one location waiting for the wind to die down so you can photograph one particular weed without blurry movement. Make the photograph, pack up your gear, drive exactly 50 yards, pull off to the side of the road again and begin to bring out all of your gear for another wonderful composition. Explain to your loving spouse that time is meaningless in the production of art and that it is not how many miles you drive, but how far your aesthetic vision is extended that determines the success of a trip. Then photograph another weed. They will understand and leave you free to travel solo on all future trips.

18. Having resigned yourself to the concept that your pursuit of creative art and any form of economics are mutually incompatible, you will begin to pursue non-profit gallery spaces who are willing to show your work for free. You will quickly discover the photographic version of the "shell game" a variation of the ever-popular "three-card Monty." In photographic terms this will appear as "send us three slides and $20 and we might include you in our upcoming juried show." Trust me on this one, three-card Monty is a lot more fun and your chances of winning are greater.

19. Ansel Adams has said that any photographer worth his salt has made 10,000 negative before his real career begins. Even then, an extraordinary year results in just 10 good images. When you are young, you will think he was a pessimist. When you are older, you will think he was an optimist.

20. Similarly, when you are young, you will think Ansel

Adams was a God. As you age, you will think he was incredibly lucky. By the time you reach your seventies, you will feel quite bitter toward him. This is a natural part of the aging process and you must trust that he will forgive you when you arrive in his heaven.

21. Workshops will be your haven. There, you will spend a week or so surrounded by fellow enthusiasts, talk shop, look at photographs, critique into the wee hours of the morning, and bond. Well, sort of. You will at least feel a warm affection for all those participants whose work is clearly inferior to your own. You will feel a vague hostility to all those whose work is clearly better than your own. You will assume no one else feels this way. In fact, everyone will – the result of which is that at the end of the workshop you will engage in a group hug of genuine affection and then never, ever see any of these people again as long as you live.

22. You will eventually die a poor, desolate artist and all of your work will be sold for 50-cents, per box, at an estate sale held in your front yard. Fifty years or so after your death, your work will be re-discovered and your career will be celebrated, applauded and widely published. Unfortunately you won't care, because you will be dead.

23. Furthermore, if your posthumous career makes you really widely known, your best artwork will be used in advertising campaigns, tourist postcards, T-shirts and computer screen savers just like the *Mona Lisa*.

The bottom line is that there is simply only one hope for art career success:

If it is fun, if it entertains you, if you would rather be making photographs than anything else, and if you truly believe that what you are doing is fundamentally unimportant, you will be guaranteed a successful art career.

If, on the other hand, you view creating your artwork as hard work, it bores you, you would rather do anything else and, most importantly, if you believe that what you are doing is important to the future of mankind, you will spend most of your life in a state of frustration, depression, and perhaps be downright suicidal. You may even cut off your ear.

So this, dear readers, is what it means to be an artist. And for all the tea in China, I wouldn't trade it for a day job.

Two

BOXES

Magritte Was A Painter

Language, undoubtedly one of humanity's most useful and inventive tools, can be such an insult. The statement, "Magritte was a painter" is terribly inadequate. It's true, he was, but his life and his art had so little to do with pigment, that to call him a painter is to insult his creative vision. Magritte was no more a painter than Paul Strand was a photographer. It is because they are not so simply defined that these two creative individuals rose to significance and were able to convey such important expression in their art.

The other day, a friend introduced me to someone with the following: "Let me introduce Brooks Jensen. He's a photographer." In just three words – "he's a photographer" – my entire career was described, explained, and dismissed. The conversation moved on with my place in the cosmic hierarchy defined.

While talking later with my new acquaintance, I learned more about how he thought of me. He explained that as a photographer, I was a certain type of individual – a gearhead, a fast talker, a motor-driven image maniac, surrounded by beautiful models, fast cars, editors and deadlines, or – at best – an ecological recluse spending all of my time in the pristine mountains photographing for calendars and postcards. This was the image contained in the definition "He's a photographer." We have all experienced this stereotyping at one time or another – that moment of truth when you announce you're a photographer and your friends and neighbors describe their most scenic memory or, as Ted Orland once prophesied, ask you to photograph their weddings.

This wouldn't be significant or worthy of comment if language did not have the power to create reality. Such observations are dangerous because they contain a hidden self-limiting box. As a workshop instructor, I've seen hundreds of portfolios from students containing innumerable photographs of trees, rivers, mountains, and patterns-in-the-sand, but I rarely see photographs that relate to their lives, thoughts, feelings or experiences.

It's been said that the role of the artist is to teach us to see and that's true. However, the role of other artists is to teach me how *they* see. To learn how *I* see, is something that cannot be taught, but must be learned. It is too easy to be the photographer that is *expected* rather than the artist *within*. It is too easy to photograph what other photographers have already taught us to see and what others have claimed to be photographically significant subject material.

When one abandons the box definitions and decides to be (or is seduced into being) an artist, then definitions are restrictions. A photographer may be, as Webster defines it, "one who photographs," but a *photographic artist* is one who observes and sees, who feels and expresses, who reacts and interprets, who listens and thinks, and responds.

I wish language was not so cumbersome, and that my friend had been able to introduce me not as "a photographer" but as "one who observes and sees, feels and expresses, reacts and interprets, listens and thinks, and responds." Unfortunately, because of language, I will probably always be referred to as a "photographer." The next time I'm introduced as a photographer, I'll try to remember what Magritte taught us in his painting, *This Is Not a Pipe*.

Symbols are nothing more than symbols. Reality is, well, you know what reality is. The important question here is not "are you a *photographer* or are you an *artist*?" There are other more important questions: What do you see? What do you feel? What do you think? What do you hear? How do you respond? Let these questions define you instead. Magritte, Paul Strand, Dvorak, Rodin, Li Po and Shakespeare deserve to be called artists because they refused to be defined by their craft. This is one of the meanings in the Chinese artist's credo *Chi Yung Sheng Tung*, "Heaven's Breath Vitalizes Movement."

Three

DAY JOBS

When Life and Art Collide

I met Ansel Adams only once, very briefly, at a gallery opening. It was at the Weston Gallery in Carmel just a few years before he died. I was one of the first in the gallery and I saw him, standing there, a big smile on his face, peering through those black-framed glasses at a giant, wall-size print of *Monolith Face of Halfdome* behind him. I shook his hand and fumbled out some feeble comment about how much I liked his work. I secretly wished he had heard about my photography and would comment about how wonderful he found my work. Hell, my parents barely knew I did photography! I vividly remember shaking his rough-gnarled, arthritic, outdoorsman's hand and feeling like I had met the Pope. It is this image of the Grand Old Man, the artistic King of Photography, that comes to mind every time I think of Ansel Adams.

Curiously enough, this same kind of imagery dominates my mental images of all the other photographers I admire. I see Wright Morris as a successful photographer in his eighties with flowing gray hair and black moustache. Brett Weston is, in my mind's eye, a bold, passionate, and lusty old man in his seventies with pipe aglow and head cocked high. Imogen Cunningham exists in my mind as a frail but mischievous elf-like figure with a twin lens reflex. Minor White is a thin, white-haired Zen guru. Edward Weston stares vacantly toward some unknown memory before he was stricken with Parkinson's disease.

I paint these images to make a point. In fact, these great photographers were *none* of these things, except perhaps fairly late in their career after they were already successful and even *famous* individuals. I've recently become more aware of the limitations of such hero worship.

Not long ago, I was speaking with a very close friend of Brett Weston. I was fascinated by the stories I heard of Weston's life. Weston confessed to my friend – late in life, after he'd become famous and successful – that for forty years he never filed an income tax report with the IRS. In *forty years* as an artist, he had never once made enough income to require him to file income tax! It's a wonderful anecdote and possibly even true. After hearing this story, I began to wonder about the realities of life as an artist. Is it fair to assume that Ansel Adams occasionally bought groceries, did the laundry, mowed the grass, played ball with the kids, argued with the neighbors, cleaned the downspouts, changed the spark plugs and shopped for socks? Did André Kertész ever wash his dishes? I suppose so. There is every reason to believe that great artists had chores like the rest of us, but it is so tempting to assume that everyone in their lives knew their artistic vision was important and historic. I see great artists as pampered, protected, sanctified individuals who were separate from the drudgery of daily life. Of course, this is not true. Great photographers are just *people*, like all of us, and subject to the same daily demands. If there is a difference between us, it is not in the basics of life but rather in our different *responses to life*.

I've always had to work for a living. I tend to use that as an excuse for the art projects I've never begun or never completed. It's been so handy to use *life* as my excuse – as though the luminaries in art didn't have such trivial details to take them away from the creation of their great works. By using this convenient myth, I can believe that I too could be creating great works of art if I didn't have to clean the fridge, commute or think about the non-art complications of life. (Unfortunately, it never occurred to me that cleaning the fridge could itself be an impetus for creating art until I had seen Josef Sudek's wonderful photographs of eggs, cheese, bread, and paper bags. Damn him for adding so powerfully to my guilt!)

What to do? If we can't change *life*, then we must change our *response* to life and see the magic of the world in which we live. Sudek photographed eggs and cheese. Wynn Bullock made *Child in Forest, 1951* while on a camping vacation with his family. The key is to integrate our art into our life, not the other way around. I once interviewed Chip Hooper who explained that he kept his camera in his car at all times and typically made photographs on his way home when the light was just right. As Ansel Adams is so often quoted in photographic circles, "Success favors the prepared mind."

Photographer David Bayles, one of the best workshop instructors around, is fond of saying that in order to create great art one has to photograph every day – *every day*. He then stresses that this doesn't mean exposing film every day or even printing every day. In order to be a great artist one must be *thinking photographically*, looking *at* photographs, looking *for* photographs, sensitive to potential photographs, rehearsing, practicing and even, when possible, creating photographs on film and paper. His point is that photography is not something that happens or should happen at special times at special places on special days or even by special people. Every day can be a day on the path of the creative life.

Why is it that so many photographers (myself included) believe that we can make important and significant artwork by working only occasionally? Athletes can't compete at the highest levels if they workout only a few times a year. Musicians, surgeons, and even tax accountants know the value of dedication and repetition. Why do we think we are different?

For me, the answer to this question is the seduction of luck. I know I can't write a great novel with luck. I can't make it to baseball's World Series with luck. I can't discover new laws of physics with luck. But I can (or so it seems) make great photographs with nothing more than an expensive camera (a myth the camera-makers love to enable) and one lucky 1/60th of a second. I know I share this feeling with a lot of photographers because I hear it expressed in workshops all the time. "I started photography because I wanted to make art but I couldn't paint. I lack the talent to sculpt. I tried drawing and all I could make were stick figures." Are we sure? Or did we give up too soon?

I'm beginning to think that photographers tend to share one consistent personality trait – photographers are *impatient*. Four minutes is a long time to wait for a print to come up in the developer. Reciprocity failure is a *failure of film manufacturing*, not a law of physics. Why can't they just make a film with an ISO of 10,000 and be done with it? We want quick-release tripod heads, faster motor drives, instant recycle times on strobes, and frames that snap together without screws. Give it to us quickly. Give it to us now. It all starts to sound like the whining of a five-year-old.

When Ansel Adams told us that in a good year he might produce 10 good photographs, maybe he was giving us advice to slow down. We misunderstood and thought he was telling us to expose even more film to increase the odds of success. Seeing takes *time*. Photographing takes *time*. Printing takes *time*. Fortunately, time is doled-out to us equally every day, equally for every one of us. Maybe the great lesson that is presented to us everyday is that there will *never* be time for photography, but there is always time for *life*. When we find a way to make photography fit our life, we'll have time for photography. Perhaps we'd best learn this before our time for life runs out.

Four

CREATIVITY & CONFUSION

I've come to the conclusion that there is considerable confusion these days in the arts community about the nature of creativity. It is currently a fad to equate creativity with *abandon* – that is to say, a *purposeful abnormality*. A great deal of art is now messy, disordered, chaotic, and distasteful. An artist throws a bucket of paint off the roof, splashes it onto a canvas a couple of stories below, it creates a giant mess and it is called "*creative*." Combine this with another common popular myth – that true creativity is somehow anti-establishment – and people start confusing *creativity* with *chaotic anarchy*.

The cloud of confusion surrounding creativity isn't easy to brush away because it is so easy to remember unconventional people who have been great artists – Lenny Bruce, Jimi Hendrix, Jackson Pollock, and Van Gogh, to name just a few. It is seductive to conclude that creativity was born from their abnormality, schizophrenia, substance abuse or anti-social behavior. Although creativity and abnormality may often go together, there is no *cause and effect relationship* between them. A *weird* individual is not necessarily a creative one, either in personality or in their artwork. Worse yet, implied in this erroneous strategy of expression is its corollary – that normalcy, manners, tact, sensitivity, and humility are somehow *not* creative. Translation: if it can be *understood*, it must not be creative.

The truth that flies in the face of this thinking is that creative vision is almost never a *mess*. Instead, it is a *clarification* of what could not be seen so easily without it. Michelangelo was creative because he saw, and then painted, what others could not. Using the same logic, Jimi Hendrix was also creative because he heard, and then performed, music that others could not. It was not his anti-social behavior that made him a creative individual. It was his talent and ability to see a new and different (albeit *complicated*) non-mess that demands our admiration, not his antics. Both of these artists distilled and clarified their vision so we could see it, too. I suppose the difficulty is in distinguishing between *mere* mess and *genius* mess.

Picasso was *avant garde* but he did not create *mess*. He created an order that might have *appeared* like a mess to those who were as yet uninitiated into his view of the world. That is to say, the art of a genius may *look* simple – or perhaps I should say like the art of a beginner – but it is not. A first grader's first attempt at a clay ash tray and a Japanese master's tea cup can both be called *simple* but they are not the same. The simplicity of genius and the simplicity of the novice are related but certainly not interchangeable.

This next statement may offend some, but I am tired of seeing crayon stick figures drawn by school age children displayed in airport lobbies as *art*. Sure, children are virtuous because of their innocence. This does not make their *artwork* virtuous. When is someone going to stand up and say, bluntly, that this is bad art? If this sounds harsh, can we at least agree that it is immature art? A child's art certainly belongs on the refrigerator as an encouragement to develop their skills, but to thrust it on the public is to insult them and to falsely delude the budding artist that *hard work* and *time* are not necessary components to *accomplishment*. Every time I see such displays, I can't help but think of the mature artists who are struggling to find an audience (or make a living) who do not "qualify" for such exposure because they are adults or, God forbid, ask for money for their artwork. A child, whose art is subsidized by their parents, does not need the subsidy of the public. The working and mature artist of accomplishment *relies* on it. Shouldn't we reward *accomplishment* rather than *potential*?

I was once thoroughly and convincingly hoodwinked by a false art guru. His art was weird, trite, amateurish and thoroughly inconsequential. Nonetheless, the power of his authority and my lack of confidence combined to convince me that his intelligence and artwork were so subtle, so deeply mysterious, so significantly *esoteric* that my failure to understand him or his artwork was only a manifestation of my own limitations. With what criteria does the initiate judge the master? True genius, he persuaded, would instantly recognize him for the mystic he claimed to be. To a naïve and insecure eighteen year old, it was a convincing argument. I now cringe when I hear such piffle offered up as a defense for inferior artwork.

Inferior artwork? There is a popular movement against such value judgments. It proposes that value judgments are meaningless in the world of art. Nonsense! That the world of art should be without standards of *quality* is ridiculous. The idea that obtuse and obscure artwork is *better* is merely an excuse. I am also tired of exhibits that offer up ill-conceived, badly executed, shallow and meaningless drivel as deep and profound artistic insights.

Do not, however, mistake my sentiment – I am not against the *new*. I am against the *banal* masquerading under the guise of the *esoteric*. Far too often there is an "in joke" quality in the piffle I see that is supposed to intimidate me into submission of my opinions before I embarrass myself by confessing my naiveté. Hogwash! Certainly my opinions are not sacrosanct, but neither are those of these artists. These artists are like the merchants selling the emperor new clothes and I refuse to be fooled by them. Honest debate is always a worthy response and passive acceptance should never be required!

We *are* so easily hoodwinked because we have forgotten that *genius* and *discipline* are the inseparable *yin* and *yang* of great art. Because the bizarre and the abnormal are so easy to achieve, producing a mess and promoting it as genius is very seductive, especially to the general, "less educated" public who will buy the concept, philosophically and commercially. Such pretense is based on blind faith in an unethical authority. Nowhere is the confusion about this more evident than so many of today's MFA programs. We judge the work *not* on its innate ability to communicate and inspire with clarity, but on the value of the MFA itself. When was the last time you read an artist's statement that *clarified* anything?

It becomes so muddled that we cannot seem to make any judgments at all anymore. *All art is virtuous when seen from a certain point of view.* How absurd. Using this logic, the actions of a gifted and loquacious liar are virtuous when considered from the point of view of a linguist because they use so effectively the language! The stick figure of a child or the mess of an incompetent adult artist are virtuous only when seen from the eyes of a public who is uneducated or unwilling to say, "This is bad."

Artwork, if it is worth anything, is about quality – quality in vision, quality in intensity, quality in *life*. The process of being an artist is nothing more than the pursuit of quality above all else. An artist who does not strive for excellence is a oxymoron. An artist who substitutes a fake experience for creative insight is a hack, a charlatan, a liar, a phony, and a cheat.

Bad art, good art – it's such a thorny issue. If what I am proposing is true, then an appropriate question might be *how can you tell the difference between true creativity and a mess?* I'm afraid this is an unanswerable question, but it is a *knowable experience.* That it cannot be accurately defined *in words* does not make it unreal. Many experiences are knowable without being describable. As Saint Augustine said when asked to give a definition of *reality,* "I *know* what it is, but when I try to *say* what it is, I don't." Similarly, I *know* when a piece of art is piffle and when it is not, even though I may not be able to *explain* it. I just wish more people would be honest about the drivel and perhaps, if we are fortunate, we could find ourselves surrounded by more artwork that is worthy of our attention.

This, in the final analysis, is what the career of an artist is all about. What separates the immature artist from the master is the developed eye, the developed hand, the trained sense of intuition (as paradoxical as that sounds), the recognition that differentiates a meaningless mess from a piece of art. Any oaf can take an old kitchen appliance, beat on it with a sledge hammer for a while, mount it on a block of walnut and call it *art*. They may even fool enough people to have a career, but it would be a dishonest career because the artist's product is nothing more than a reflection of an artist's *mind* and *life*. A shallow mind, a shallow life, will produce shallow art work. No amount of manipulative shenanigans can disguise a lack of genuine creativity. Purposeful messes cannot disguise a lack of deeper insight. If we are to clarify the confusion about the current bad artwork, it must begin with an honest appraisal and the courage to speak with conviction when rubbish is exhibited as genius. We must not be so afraid of a difference of opinion that we are willing to sacrifice quality in our values for harmonious banality.

Five

ONE HUNDRED PRINTS

It starts with, "That little corner in the basement could work…" or, "The extra bathroom could be converted easily enough." These simple thoughts are precursors to building your own darkroom. But, this tempting path is longer and more treacherous than you might initially guess.

For example, the minute you have your own darkroom, all of your friends and neighbors will now perceive you as a photographer. At parties you will no longer be introduced as "John Doe – he works for XYZ Company." You will now be introduced as "John Doe – he is a photographer." As Ted Orland has joked, suddenly you will be invited on a regular basis to photograph weddings – for free. "Bring your camera," will become code for "You're not invited because we enjoy your personality and desire your companionship, but rather because we'd like someone to record this event and we've volunteered you involuntarily."

All of this can be endured or creatively avoided – all except the deadly question, "May I see some of your work?" I used to dread that question; I hated that question. It forced me to confront the (capital P) Problem of (capital C) Completion. It's frankly *embarrassing* to be introduced as a photographer when you know in your heart that you have not produced enough photographs. There is so little satisfaction in showing your negatives, your contact sheets, your test strips, and your unmounted, un-spot-toned, roughly printed work prints.

"I'm not quite done with this one."

"I'm not sure that this one says exactly what I mean."

"This is still a work-in-progress."

"The next time I print this one, I'm going to make the following changes … "

"Now if you could just imagine that this part was printed just a little darker, and this part was printed a little lighter, and that thing in the background wasn't there, this thing was sharply focused, and that the edges were cropped a little differently, and that it was mounted and framed, then you'd know exactly what I'm working towards."

I hated that question. Pretty soon, you are being introduced as "John Doe – a friend I've known for a long time." You know it's an introduction that they've chosen out of kindness because what they *really* wanted to say was " – a guy who pretends to be a photographer, but hasn't done anything for years and years and years, and we all have doubts about whether he's capable, serious, talented, or worthy of continued existence on the planet." You know the moment of truth has arrived. It's time to produce or sell the darkroom equipment and convert the basement into a ping-pong rec-room.

The reason I can write about this so convincingly is because, quite honestly, I've lived it. For the first fifteen years I was involved with photography, I was not a *photographer*. I was, in reality, merely a dabbler, a dilettante, at best a student of photography. I tested, learned, practiced, attended workshops, printed and then reprinted the same image over and over again, and struggled desperately to figure out what the hell the Zone System was all about. In all of this work, intense as it was, I didn't create a single print that I would proudly show today. And, so, when someone asked to see my work, I blanched, shuffled my feet and talked about how close I was to understanding DlogE curves and the circle of confusion.

It's not that I had never produced *any* work, but the work I produced was, well, eclectic. If I had been asked to exhibit a show, I would have shown several different styles, on at least a dozen different papers, with four or five different mat boards, a half a dozen different matting techniques and – in short – a hodgepodge of work that would have been more convincing if it had been produced by two dozen photographers.

I've discussed this dilemma with a number of photographers and discovered that I'm not alone. In fact, I'd say this is the rule rather than the exception in work that I see at photography workshops. Luckily, I stumbled onto a way out.

My moment of truth came in 1989 when I had some extended time off – a period of about six weeks – in which I had the opportunity to contemplate an extended darkroom project. I had recently been asked (again) to show some of my work and (again) begged off. I considered the situation for a while and then decided it was time to put up or shut up. I decided to spend six weeks engaged in what I called *The 100 Prints Project*. The project was founded in the faith that after 15 years of taking pictures, certainly in all of my boxes of negatives there had to be 100 negatives worth printing as completed, finished, exhibitable artwork. The objective was to print, tone, spot, mat and finish 100 prints that would become my core work. If anyone asked to "see my work" I'd be ready. It seemed like a simple, straightforward objective with a precisely definable goal and time frame. I did *not* see the true benefit of dedicating myself to this project until it was over.

Here are a few of my observations and the lessons I learned.

My first decision was a practical one: I was not going to use any of this time to photograph. Ansel Adams once said that a photographer was doing well if he produced ten decent photographs a year. Having been involved in photography for fifteen years, I calculated that I could be inefficient by a factor of one-third and still have a hundred prints just waiting to be completed.

Lesson #1 – Organization

I turned to my negative files to begin the process of selecting the negatives I would print. Here, before I even began, was my first lesson. I had rolls and rolls of undeveloped film and old shoe boxes piled up with negatives poorly stored and not even contact printed. I didn't even know what I *had!* I quickly realized that, just like almost any other aspect of life, organization is the first step to success. I spent a week (and more than a few dollars on Light Impressions supplies) just filing negatives, making contact prints and organizing my collection of negatives so I could see what I had. It was a lesson well-learned. I now keep my negative files orderly and contact print every roll immediately after developing it. I am fastidious about properly filing and archiving my digital files. Perhaps it's a simplistic truth, but if you can't *find* the negative/file you need, it's going to be tough to make a decent print of it.

Lesson #2 – Hit ratio

Because I wanted to print 100 finished prints in the project, I decided to inspect contact sheets and file prints to select 150 good-looking negatives. I estimated that I might abandon as much as one third of the negatives because, after printing them, I would discover they were simply unprintable to the quality I wanted. I was right, except that I overestimated my success rate. Toward the end of the six weeks, I had to dig deeper into my negative files to come up with a hundred prints to finish the project.

The biggest lesson I learned at this stage was one that effected my *photographing* more than my printing: *film is cheap.* After spending the time and money to get somewhere to photograph; after lugging all that equipment over hill and dale; after coming home, developing the film and making the contact print, it's stupid and frustrating to lose an image because you didn't bracket the exposure, because the wind blew at the wrong moment, because you should have used f/32 instead of f/16, or because a piece of fuzz caught the film plane inside your camera. In other words, it's folly to make one exposure in the field and count on it to excel. If it's worth making one exposure, it's worth making a few, a bracketed exposure or two and a back up. If the subject is not worth this much film, move on.

I also learned it's a good idea to check the image again after the exposures are made, just in case you've accidentally moved the focus, kicked the tripod leg, or vignetted the corners with the lens hood.

Lesson #3 – Style

I started printing by grabbing a negative at random and diving in. Of course, the very first act after placing the negative in the enlarger, demanded a decision. How high do I crank the enlarger head, i.e., how big should I make the print? This decision was quickly followed by a multitude of others: What paper should I use? What is the right paper color? What is the right mat board? What is the right mounting technique? What is the right presentation style?

After making just a few prints I realized I was headed down a path that would result in 100 prints on a variety of papers in an assortment of sizes on different mat boards with different mounting techniques – again. Such an assortment does not create *a cohesive body of work*. By not standardizing a bit, it was easy to get bogged down quickly in a plethora of decisions that diverted my attention from the true task at hand – making a print that looked like it fit into a larger body of work.

By limiting my choices to one print size (with some variations for cropping), one paper (in my case, Ilford Multi-Grade Fiber Base), one toning technique, one brand of mat board, and one style of presentation, I found I was able to sidestep making these complicated decisions over and over again.

Admittedly, this is unfairly restrictive for the accomplished, experienced, and masterful photographer. But that was not the nature of this project nor the nature of my experience at that point. This project was one that I engaged in at a time in my career when such decisions were overwhelming. One of my early teachers advised me to stick with one film and one developer combination and to learn it well rather than bounce from film to film, developer to developer, paper to paper. He was absolutely right. It doesn't seem like it should be good advice, but it is. I don't know a single accomplished photographer who advocates a scattered approach as the best way to learn photography.

Lesson #4 – Print for a purpose

One of the problems I quickly discovered was the challenge of printing for a purpose. When you go into the darkroom to simply make a print, questions such as size, toning, finishing, etc. are whimsical decisions. As I mentioned above, carried on with repetition, you will eventually have an eclectic body of work that doesn't hang together with a sense of polished completion. In order to print with a purpose, you need to choose the eventual use of the print *before* you begin printing. If the print is intended as a stand-alone presentation above the fireplace, a certain set of printing disciplines are invoked. If the print will be part of a portfolio, then it demands a different set of printing decisions. In essence, I learned that if you don't have a purpose in mind before you start printing, then questions about how to print are overwhelmingly unanswerable.

By deciding that my purpose for this printing project was to have one-hundred similarly matted and finished works to show, I defined a look that I was then able to execute consistently. Individual decisions could be made *in the context of the overall project*.

Learning this lesson alone made the *100 Prints Project* worth the effort. Now, other than file prints and work prints, I don't even begin a darkroom session until I have thought through the purpose for the print and the context in which it will be seen. A somewhat simplistic example of this thought process is learned from Paul Strand. He defined the type of light his prints were supposed to be viewed in before he began printing! He would make prints for specific gallery lighting conditions, often dictating what the lighting conditions would be where he could. In other words, is difficult to know which route to take when you don't know your destination.

Lesson #5 – Learning to see

As it turned out, I printed 121 finished prints but kept only 103 finished pieces in the final cut. It seems silly that I didn't anticipate it, but after I had finished the first 50 or so prints, my admiration for the first dozen began to deteriorate. *The more*

I printed, the more I learned how to print. To be more accurate, the more I printed, the more I developed the ability to *see* what was on the paper. Some of the early prints, I either reprinted or threw out.

Fred Picker mentioned an exercise that he did as a beginning photographer that involved printing around a hundred continuous tone patches in an attempt to create as many gray steps between black and white as he possibly could. He talks about some grays being harmonious with one another; some tones being sweet and some discordant, and some tones being "right" and some tones being "off." I had no idea what he was talking about until I engaged in my *100 Prints Project* and found, to my amazement, that my ability to see black and white tones improved dramatically as I worked my way through the 100 prints. I am convinced that had I not undertaken this project, I would have never learned how to print – and see – black and white.

Lesson #6 – *The value of experience*

Repetition is a virtue. Repetition is a virtue. If this is true for athletes and musicians, why wouldn't it be true for photographers, too? The *100 Prints Project* taught me lots of little things that might have taken me years to learn. I learned things like: Sandstone is very difficult to print well; slightly filtered sunlight looks better than direct sun; a small beautiful print is better than a big ugly one; the most important part of designing your darkroom is the light by which you choose to view and judge wet prints and test-strips; it's possible to give up on a negative too early; it's more likely you will continue to work with a bad negative for far too long; spot-toning is a distant second-best solution, it is better to meticulously clean the negative; Durst makes spectacularly functional enlargers; Saunders makes the best four-bladed easels, and the list could go on almost indefinitely.

Lesson #7 – *Working through "the compulsories"*

Of all these small lessons garnered by the experience, the most important and most unexpected was that I was not *nearly* as interested in photographing certain subject matter as I thought I was. It is easy to start off as a photographer, photographing what you *think* you are supposed to photograph rather than what you are truly internally inspired to photograph. Printing 100 prints of subjects about which you have limited passion is a good way to cure yourself of photographing compulsories.

Lesson #8 – Format

The word photographer should be a *verb*. A painter is one who paints. A photographer is *one who photographs*. But to stop at that comparison is too simplistic. Once a painter has painted, he or she is, for all intents and purposes, *done*. Oh, maybe a frame needs to be added, but essentially, the final brush stroke is the end of the painter's creative act. Nothing could be further from the truth for the photographer. Clicking the shutter – that is, the act of actually taking the photograph – is not even a decent beginning. At some point, you will still need to develop the film, print it, tone it, mat it, and then frame it.

In my *100 Prints Project*, one of the oddest revelations was that even *that* assumption was subject to question. Who says the ultimate destination for a photograph is the mat board, frame and *wall*? The farther I got into the project, the more I found myself printing personal images rather than *copies* of the old masters. The more I worked on these personal images, the more I got in touch with my own intentions and subconscious visions for my work.

I started questioning how some of the images I loved were going to look on the wall. The more I thought about it, the more I realized that a considerable number of photographs demonstrating my vision had nothing to do with wall art décor. This led me to think about alternatives that I had never before considered. It was in the midst of the *100 Prints Project* that I found myself thinking about publications, portfolios, artist's books, keepsakes, bookmarks, *tanzaku* (a Japanese form of paper wind-poem that hangs in trees), and small, intimate prints.

Conclusions

It is not an original observation that practice makes perfect or that experience is the greatest teacher. The problem with this homily is that it's *not true* – at least not as true as it could be. The cold hard fact is that practice does *not* make perfect. Rather, it is the practice of *perfection* that makes perfect. Many beginning photographers have spent a considerable number of years tinkering and dabbling and pooping around in the darkroom and I was among them. It was only when I dedicated myself to producing 100 prints, as perfect as I could make them, that I really made progress in my photographic skills. But, it was more than that. Yes, I'd learned a great deal about craft, but I'd also learned some valuable lessons about my photographic eye, interests, and other insights that I would have never predicted as benefits of the *100 Prints Project*.

My *100 Prints Project* was, in retrospect, one of the turning points in my photographic career. Had I never engaged in this project, I'm convinced that my photography would today be significantly hampered. It was such a powerful turning point in my career that I've made this project a recommendation to a number of students in my workshops.

After it was all done, the net result of my project was 103 finished, matted, exhibitable prints; a major leap forward in craft skills, and an insight into a whole new direction I could take my photographic artwork. That's not a bad harvest for a guy who was essentially trying to avoid embarrassment.

THE IMPORTANCE
OF STRUCTURE

In another essay I discussed my *100 Prints Project* and the lessons I learned when I made the commitment to produce 100 finished, mounted photographs in six short weeks. One of the lessons I learned in that project was the importance of *structure*. In this essay, I'd like to expand on that theme.

When I began the *100 Prints Project*, one of the first things I realized was that I would need to restrict some of the variables involved in the production of each individual image. For example, what size should each image be? What paper should I use for each image? What toning was appropriate for that image? By considering all of these questions on each individual image, I quickly recognized that the final style of the project would be discontinuous and not hold together as a unified body of work. Then, I decided to limit those variables and did so by printing each image to approximately the same size, on the same paper, with the same toning, and mounted the same way. Once I had made *that* decision, producing the body of work became considerably easier, and the finished prints were similar enough to be exhibited as a unified body of work.

Writing about this now makes this decision seem easy, almost flippant. It was not. In fact, I sweated bullets over these decisions because I knew that they were the foundation against which the entire structure of the project depended. The obvious construction analogy is not only useful but it is quite accurate: *Without a good solid structural foundation, a building collapses.*

I believe the same can be said about a body of work, and even about an artist's career.

It's the weekend and it's time to make art. Don't laugh – this is a common scenario for most artmakers. So what are you going to do with your artmaking time this weekend? Far too often the answer is "begin." Photographers head to the field or studio with camera in hand, or perhaps into the darkroom with new negatives to print. Painters gather materials, stretch canvas, and start looking for something to paint. It's the same for all artists, writers, and creative types. Most of the time we start with a lengthy session of cleaning, organizing, preparing, and general fussing about. Although this is a manifestation of creative procrastination, at least it can be said that we start with *something* creative.

Eventually some muse speaks, however softly and impotently. We engage in a flurry of artmaking, time runs out, and Monday finds us back at work. Next weekend, it's the same program. Even with experienced and professional artmakers, I've found this to be a common, frustrating situation.

Having struggled with this scenario for years, interspersed with occasional bursts of productive creativity, I've discovered a useful pattern in a my own artmaking. Advice based on personal experience is often uselessly biased and tends to say more about the person offering the advice than provide much of use but, it may be worth sharing.

Plainly speaking, I simply don't do well without structure. When I drive, I prefer lines on the road; when writing, I keep a dictionary handy; I tend to read instruction manuals; I'm confused by a new idea until I see the pattern in which it fits. Structure is also useful in my photography. I can be much more productive when I define a project and then set about the task of executing it. When the definition is missing, the execution tends to be random, unfinished, inconsistent, and mostly theoretical. I suppose I wish I was more free-flowing, more spontaneous. That I am *not* is plain to all who know me. To ignore this would simply complicate my work. One of the keys to success is to frankly face our limitations and work within them. As the Army slogan says, "Be all you *can* be." It does not say "Be that which it is *impossible* for you to be."

So, I think in terms of projects. A project might explore a specific idea or a photographic concept may develop as a result of something I see or think. But, in order to make this project a reality, I have to begin by defining it. I first determine the eventual *use* for the final product. Is it something for the marketplace? If so, I think in terms of editions, marketability, scale, and costs. Is it something I see as a unique, single artifact? If so, I'm free to think about Polaroids, hand-colored work, gifts, and even techniques that are destructive to my negatives. Is this destined for the wall or for a book? This helps me determine which camera to use, the scale of the images relative to the detail, tonal clarity, graininess, and other factors. Essentially, by determining the final use before I begin, I can effectively reverse engineer the project for success.

Next, I think about the scope of the project. How many total images will/should this project include? One? Ten? 100? This helps me think about how many photographic sessions I will need to schedule, how many negatives I will need to expose, if the project will be produced from my existing negative archive or if it requires new photographs. If I see the project including lots of images, this immediately defines what kind of exhibition space I will seek, too.

The thousands of variables that compose any project are far too numerous to consider here. But, I often find myself asking the same *kinds* of questions with each new project. Will I include text? Will this project be produced in more than one medium – for example, multimedia, printed form, or original photographs? Is there an audience who will appreciate this work? Where will I find them? Will they be willing to pay for the privilege of seeing this work? Or do I need to pay them for the privilege of showing it?

All of these questions become a part of the project's structure. Once the project is defined, it's not cast in cement. It can be changed, modified, scrapped, restarted, or completed – after all, this is *personal* artwork, not a commercial assignment. (Although, I will admit that some of these techniques can be used in thinking through commercial assignments and are often second-nature to experienced commercial photographers.) Where I find this idea of structure most useful is in the control and expenditure of my limited artmaking time. Let's be honest, time is a rare commodity, especially for those of us who have jobs, families, responsibilities, and other pesky realities. With a defined project structure, I find it easier to assign myself specific tasks that move the project along – session by session, weekend by weekend.

I am a pragmatist about this. If I were omniscient, I could accurately project exactly how many hours of my creative life would be required to produce a final photographic project. Yet, even if I could allocate hours exactly, it would not change the concept. It would only change my *knowledge* about it. There is a finite number of hours of thought, tinkering, sweat, and craft that will be required in order for any project to be completed. I may not know how much time is required, but I do know, with absolute certainty, that the only way to reach the end is to begin and do the work. The structure of the project helps in this process. Even if the structure is modified or abandoned, having it in place makes *beginning* and *progressing* considerably more possible – and a lot more fun.

Seven

THE MAGIC OF IT

A number of years ago, I was visiting the Art Institute of Chicago specifically to see a Paul Strand exhibition. While walking down the large hallway from the main building to the back complex where the exhibit was located, I walked past a large display of medieval suits of armor. I'd never had much interest in medieval things, but I found myself absolutely mesmerized by these suits of armor. After studying them for some time, it dawned on me that what made them exquisite works of art was the intricate detail – *unbelievably* intricate detail – that went into the craft and production of each suit of armor. My mind boggled with a sense of *disbelief.* At that moment, I realized that this amazement is the magic in a great deal of artwork – you look at it and simply can't believe someone could make it. It's as though the artist did something that is not humanly possible. It was, literally, impossible; yet, there it was.

If the artist can't do it, yet it has been done, then how? As the mind reels in front of such works of art, only one conclusion makes any sense: it must be the work of the gods, of the muse, of some supernatural force working *through* the artist. Mozart created wonderful sonatas, beautiful music beyond mere musical notes. Beethoven composed subtly nuanced symphonies although he was deaf. Rembrandt used brushes made of goat hair and paint pigment made from the most primitive materials and yet painted renditions of people that look as though they are absolutely alive. *This* is the magic of it. Ordinary materials, ordinary mortals, achieving truly extraordinary results.

For us photographers: *Where's the magic?* Ansel Adams once had magic in his prints because we looked at his black and white images and said, "My God, how the hell does he do that?" Our images didn't look like his. No photograph we'd ever seen looked like his. We drooled and signed up for the workshops.

Fast forward to today. Thousands of photographers can make a beautiful, zone-and-tone print that looks every bit as good as an Adams original. Dmax and the Zone System are no longer mysteries. Photoshop and the computer are making it even easier, and soon everyone will be able to make a great photograph – well, at least a *technically* great photograph. This is, and always has been, the problem with photography as an art form. It doesn't look very magical; in fact, it looks downright mechanical. That's why there is such a natural aversion in so many traditional photography circles to the digital print; it's even *more* mechanical.

How many times have you been at a gallery opening (perhaps of your own work) and overheard someone say, "I could do that" or "I've got one better than that." Photography is billed as the *democratic* art form and everyone believes it. So how does a photographer separate their work from the lucky hobbyist? If the hobbyist has access to mechanical tools that make their images technically indistinguishable from the Master, then what is the difference?

At this point, we find a fork in the road. What is it that distinguishes fine art photography from merely making pictures? Is it subject matter or is it process – process in the complete sense of technical, mental, and spiritual?

If it is subject matter, I believe it is a shallow art form. As such, it will always struggle to be accepted (and purchased) as an equal to the traditional arts. Simply put, a lot of fine art photography has degenerated to photographing subject material that ordinary people simply do not have access to. A great deal of what passes for fine art photography today is not based on vision, talent or craft; it is based simply on *access*. Consider the plethora of books about Japanese fetish girls, portraits of indigenous peoples from the far reaches of the globe, weird rock formations, obscure and odd subcultures, or taboo subjects. The average person doesn't have access to these oddities and, therefore, can't photograph them.

This formula for success is clear. If you want to be published, find something no one else has access to and get to work. Visit the photography section of the bookstore and test my theory. You'll see that I'm right.

But, is this a solid foundation for meaningful artwork? Is this really the key? Do the best painters have access to colors denied to the ordinary painter? Are the best musicians granted access to notes ordinary musicians can't use? Are the best poets the ones with unique words? Are the photographers most worthy of publication and exhibition those with the most obscure and unfamiliar subjects?

Or, are the best artists those who use ordinary materials and ordinary subjects to create extraordinary artwork? The medieval armor I saw at the museum was just metal – not even obscure or rare metals. Picasso painted with ordinary paints; Robert Frost used ordinary words; Benny Goodman used an ordinary clarinet. (And yes, he was an *artist!*) Is it possible that the best art is a result of those who bring to the work the best craftsmanship, the clearest vision, the truest spirit, the most creative mind, the most inspired talent, and the most diligent work ethic? Hmmm ...

There is no new subject material for photography. Whatever we think is new, is actually not new at all. Worse, even somewhat new subjects are quickly reduced to fashionable or out-of-fashion trends. There was a time when the f/64 Group were considered revolutionary visionaries because they saw the "straight landscape" as subject material. Now their work seems somewhat dated and cliché. Any photographer today who tries to show us beautiful black and white images of Yosemite is considered a minor copyist and a hack. But are there no new images that can ever be made in Yosemite? Is Yosemite off-limits to photographers now? Is it Yosemite or the photographer who manifests this limitation?

There is nothing new under the sun, not really. Technologies are new, yes, but the basic human condition has not changed for thousands of years. The same passions rule us that ruled early man. The same questions plague us that have plagued our ancestors from time immemorial. This is, and always has been, the source of great art. *Who am I? Where is this place? Why?* (The philosopher Alan Watts has proposed there are only four great questions that have plagued man forever: 1.) *Who started it?* 2.) *Where's it going?* 3.) *How will it end?* 4.) *Who's going to clean it up?*)

It seems that photography presents us with a choice unique in the field of art. We can work to find something new that has never been photographed before and claim it as our unique photographic turf or we can accept the challenge to use our tools as merely tools and realize that the real task of being a photographer is to develop ourselves as conduits for the inspiration that creates artwork. One path leads to tomorrow's clichés. The other path leads to artwork that seems to endure. One eventually is easy; one is profound.

Photography is unique when compared to many traditional art media because it is ensnared in this question. Photography is the most technological of all media. The technology of photography is seductive. It's even fun! But, if we hope to make art with our tools, the issues that should command our attention are not technological. They are the issues of wonderment, mystery and depth. We are not making suits of armor. Our tools will never dazzle the viewer with their technical brilliance – at least not for long. Future generations will look back at our prints, our books, our techniques and our tools with the same quaint smile that we use when considering albumen prints and wet plates. They will never wonder how we did it; they will wonder how we could suffer through such primitive techniques.

And this is where the life of the photographic artist begins. Our work will either entertain the audience in its technological coarseness or cultural historicity, or it will engage them in the deeper questions of life. Our work will either show them our world or ask them about theirs.

This is precisely why I love photography. It is a tool, but it is also a challenge that constantly forces me to think about what I am doing, what I am making, and why.

Eight

Beyond What It Is

The old maxim advises, "Never discuss religion or politics." What the heck, let's break the rules.

All religions have two distinct sets of teachings – the *exoteric* and the *esoteric*. The exoteric teachings are highly visible and easily understandable by the masses: they are taught from the pulpit of every neighborhood church. The esoteric teachings are more subtle – known by mystics, masters and religion's deepest thinkers – and sometimes by the artists.

Photography is similar, containing both exoteric and esoteric versions. For the purposes of illustration only, it's useful to think about the exoteric and the esoteric at opposite ends of the same line. If we place the exoteric on the far left (e.g., the product catalog photo), then what kind of photography exists at the esoteric end of the line? This is an important question – particularly for many creative artists – because we tend so often to focus on the esoteric, the deep and significant image that is supposed to go beyond mere photographic recording. But what is it? This is not an academic question. Think of it this way: *What is it that makes your artwork meaningful?*

There is an old photographic maxim that goes, "If you can't make a *great* photograph of a *mundane* subject, at least make a *mundane* photograph of a *great* subject!" However, this advice often leads to the *mere reproduction* of a great subject, in this example, Nature's splendor. (As a friend of mine says each time he sets up his tripod, "Ain't Nature grand!") They are still *exoteric* photographs in that they are photographs about the objects *in front of* the camera lens. When a photograph is used to simply show what something looks like at a particular place and at a particular time, it serves primarily as a *memory device*. It either reminds us of something we've already seen or shows us something new that we will need to remember later. When the need arises, it's useful to be able to remember a recipe, a phone number, or the formula for computing the area of a circle. But such statistics and data do not make our life more *meaningful*, they simply make it *easier*.

When photography goes beyond merely showing us appearance and starts, instead, to show us something of life's deeper soul, then it approaches the esoteric. An argument could be successfully made that this is *exactly* what Ansel Adams' photographs do, even though on the surface they might look simply like pretty pictures of a pretty place. They are more. He showed us Yosemite's *soul*, not merely its rocks. (Or at the very least he showed us the Yosemite we'd all like to believe in – which says something about *our* soul!)

Edward Weston talked about photographing "the thing itself"; Minor White told his photography students, "Don't photograph simply what it *is*, rather, photograph what *else* it is." The esoteric image shows us the subject matter in a relationship of significance, shows us that the subject is worthy of noticing, or opens a door to perception, understanding, or insight that was previously closed to us.

Simply put, the importance of the exoteric photograph is the world *outside you*; the importance of the esoteric photograph is the world *inside you and inside the subject*. (This completes the course in post-post-modernist art.)

But there is quicksand here that brings me to the central point of my comments. Too many budding artists, when they discover this line of thinking, then conclude that the best esoteric (read *inner*) photography is somehow the most *personal* – and the subsequent photographs suffer. (Or more properly said, those of us who must *look* at these photographs suffer!)

The problem with most inner-driven photographs is that they are incredibly self-indulgent and self-referencing. They are a closed circle with no outside reference, no point of entry. As I write this in the first year of the new millennium, we are in the midst of an insignificant phase in the history of photography in which self-indulgent photographs are all the rage. Everyone seems to think they need psychotherapy and are using photography as a means of self-exploration, self-analysis, and self-cleansing. The resulting images are thrust on an unsuspecting public, who is then told by stupid art critics that the work is significant and meaningful. (Breathe!) In truth, these photographs *are* significant, but *only* to the individual who created them as therapy. To the rest of us, such images are merely a look at the other person's therapy. More often than not – far, far more often than not – these are boring photographs by good people, with good intentions but misdirected creativity.

Well, if the most esoteric photograph is not the most self-directed, then what is it? The answer to this question has been answered the same way throughout history. Simply said, the creation of art passes into a different plane when it ceases to be focused on *self* and instead starts focusing on *Self*. Which brings me back to religion.

It makes no difference whether you consider Self to be The Great Oneness of All Beings, God, Buddha, Nature, or (to quote G. K. Chesterton) "the which than which there is no whicher." When the subject of art becomes bigger than oneself – when the subject becomes the Universal Self (I'll use this as a catch-all phrase for God), or at least the universal self (that which we all share in our more earthly existence), it becomes a much better thing. This is not to say photography must be about religious themes, but it is always better when it is infused with a *universal component* that allows the audience entrance into the image through their ability to internalize or personally relate to the subject. I love Ansel Adams' photograph of Yosemite from the Wawona turn-out, not because I see *him* standing there, but because I can see Yosemite as though *I* was standing there.

His photographs succeed because every one of us can see ourselves looking through his eyes. In order to do this, he developed
the skill to see through ours.

It is an elusive challenge in photography, but it is not impossible. Edward Weston captured it with his shells, his peppers,
and his dead pelicans; André Kertész captured it in a single vase
and flower in *Chez Mondrian*, and Alfred Eisenstaedt captured
it in *Kiss, V-J Day, 1945*. Such photographs contain a *universality*
that is testament to the old wisdom, "Do not speak unless spoken
through."

As far back as ancient Greece, artists have talked about
the muse or the daemon that speaks *through* the artist to all mankind. I suspect that before the world of electronics, the world was
a quieter place and the muse was more easily heard. Nowadays,
most artists have to work very hard just to catch a whisper, a hint,
or even a wink from the muse. How does the subject want to be
photographed? What is the Universe trying to say through you
in this image? Can you see this image you are about to make
through the eyes of the rest of humanity? What will they see
and will it make a difference? Can you photograph your subject
through another's eyes?

The difficulty with these questions – other than the obvious
risk of over-analyzing your work while you're photographing – is
the necessary sense of *letting go of control*. It is not about what
you see; it is not about what you feel. If this is all it is about, then
your photographs will be of interest only to you. Can you let go
of yourself and let your subject speak directly to your audience?

In Japan it is said that an individual who has complete control
of his medium is not quite a master. The true master is one who,
indeed, has total control *and then lets go and allows an accident
to happen*. In Zen, they talk about painting with *mu-shin* which
means "no mind." This does not mean merely *thoughtless* painting,
but rather letting go of forcing it, ceasing to control it through
an act of personal will. Great artists can do this. Examples are
found in the paintings of Mark Toby, the photographs of Brett
Weston, the calligraphy of Sengai, or even the dialogs of Mark

Twain. Every writer knows there is a point at which the characters take over the plot and the task of writing changes from one of creation to one of observation. If you want to become a better photographer, become a more practiced observer and then get out of your way.

If you can find it, take a careful look at a book by Christian Vogt titled, *In Camera*. In a studio, photographer Vogt placed a large, square wooden box and asked a series of women to come and pose with the box for him in any way they chose. He let go of control. He made no suggestions and did not impose any limitations. His job was to simply record what these women chose to show of themselves. It's one of the most fascinating studies of psychology and personal expression I've ever seen. It's also a wonderful photographic portfolio.

Another classic example of observing and listening are the still life photographs of Josef Sudek. He created an entire body of work consisting of photographs of what one can't help but suspect was simply his lunch — an egg, a glass of water, and a crumpled tissue around a slice of cheese. They are wonderful photographs. It's easy to see him sitting down to this simple lunch when suddenly – a moment of revelation! The light, the shapes, the shadows! He forgets lunch and makes a wonderful photograph. My vision of how Sudek's photographs were created may be total fantasy. But for me, the pictures are more than just eggs, cheese and a glass of water. Instead, they have a movement, rhythm and story that makes them successful – not just as mere images, but as a connection directly to Sudek and his experience. A photograph that merely shows me what an egg looks like would be boring. What makes these photographs succeed is that they are not pictures of eggs. They are pictures of a *moment* – cosmic revelation or simply enjoying a meal. He listened and his muse spoke.

Listening, seeing, going beyond the limits of a subject and photographing the universal – *that* is the path of the artist.

Nine

How to Make
a Workshop Work

Every year in the three months between December and February, if you are on anyone's mailing list, you will receive brochures for everyone's photography workshops. I have a few thoughts about workshops based on my experiences as both an attendee and as an instructor.

First, let me say that this is an article in support of workshops. You should attend them. I make this as a blanket statement to every reader, regardless of their level of work or experience. The simple and unarguable truth is that workshops are the best stimulus for new work and personal growth, short of receiving a huge grant or learning about impending death!

Photography is an art and art is a personal expression. As we grow, our craft can grow. Notice – I did not say that it *would* grow – I said that it *can* grow. For it to grow, the workshop needs to encourage and foster growth.

For most of us, this is a symbiotic relationship. Our personal growth can fuel our photography and our photography can fuel our personal growth. It is necessary, however, to place ourselves into an environment that is conducive to growth – particularly one outside our daily habits and comfortable surroundings.

When you show your work to family and friends, you can predict glowing compliments and enthusiastic acceptance. This response is surely welcome. But, if we limit ourselves to this consistent "warm fuzzy," we risk becoming repetitious and blinded. We miss the chance to grow.

Show your work at a gallery and you can anticipate criticism. This may range from pinpoint insight that accurately disassembles your efforts with precision or that ever-present criticism, "I think this would look a lot better in color." Exhibition is both flattering and devastating. It isn't necessarily productive or conducive to growth.

Workshops overcome the limitations of both of these traditional institutions. A workshop offers insight and criticism, but from a caring group of fellow workers. Most participants know enough to offer blunt yet compassionate advice. With luck, your instructors can help, too.

I attended my first photographic workshop in 1982. Since then, I have attended a couple dozen more. I've also taught a dozen or so workshops. I've been fortunate to learn from some excellent teachers and fellow students. I've also suffered through some awful presentations by accomplished photographers.

Based on my own experiences, I can offer a few ideas about workshops. I hope they may motivate you to attend another (or your first!) workshop. At the least, I hope they help make your workshop experience more productive.

Reasons To Attend A Workshop

Reason #1: The instructor(s)

Choose your workshop based on the instructor(s) rather than the location, cost, topic, or agenda. It is always the instructor's wisdom, teaching skill and abilities that determine the workshop's success. Notice, I did *not* say the photographer's *work* should determine your choice. Just because someone can make a good photograph does not mean they can *teach*. Far too often, workshop attendees are disappointed by a photographer whose work they admire, but whose teaching skills make the workshop a disaster. (See the final caution at the end of this article.)

Reason #2: To elevate your peer level

In your neighborhood, there may not be any photographers of merit. If you're lucky, your town may hold a few dozen, your state, a few more. Workshops bring these geographically divergent people together. It is the best way to meet others who are as dedicated and committed to the craft as you are, no matter what your dedication or commitment level. At the workshop, you will likely find "kindred spirits" who share your perspective. These can, and often do, develop into significant friendships.

Reason #3: See the teacher's work

Every workshop instructor worth their salt brings at least 200 of their own photographs to show students, both in formal and informal presentations. If they bring only slides of their printed work, choose a different workshop.

The opportunity to see their work, up close and unhurried, is one of the greatest advantages of a workshop. Galleries tend to show only finished, published, sellable, "greatest hits," or famous work. At workshops, you will usually see a much broader assortment than is possible in a gallery. The better workshop instructors even bring failures, works-in-progress, raw prints and, occasionally, negatives. This is often the most valuable experience of a workshop.

Here are the four questions to ask: How did they overcome the limitations of the negative? How did they get to where they are from where they began? Why did they make those choices? How did they know to make those choices? These are not questions easily answered in books or gallery presentations.

Reason #4: See the good work of other workshop students

It seems there is always at least one student whose work is as good as the teacher's – or better! If they are beginning their career this work may be unfamiliar or unpublished, or occasionally the student is simply too shy to exhibit it. Workshop exposure may be the only way to see their fine work. Incidentally, these are people with whom you can often make great print trades.

Reason #5: Increase your work volume prior to attending

At a workshop, we all want to put our best foot forward and show our best work. For most of us, our best work is still yet to be done. We don't want to show the limited work we have in a box in the closet! So, we jump into the darkroom before the workshop to make new work to show. If the workshop merely provides motivation for this work, it's probably worth it.

Reason #6: Develop additional written resources

At all good workshops, you will receive a suitcase full of distributed materials. This is because a good teacher knows that there is so much more to teach than time will allow *and* that every student will only hear what they are currently prepared to hear. Distributing written resources overcomes these limitations.

Reason #7: Books, magazines, galleries, other workshops

I think the current buzzword is *resource development*. There are lots of great materials out there and you might have missed something of interest. Workshops are a great resource to learn what's out there that might be useful to you.

Reason #8: Guilt yourself into post-workshop work

See an increase in the volume of your work as mentioned in Reason #5 above.

Reason #9: Pick up new mechanical techniques

This is a misunderstood *biggie*. Most people place great importance on the new techniques they will learn. Sure, this is a reason to attend, but it should be a relatively minor reason. Most techniques have been published and can be studied easily without attending a workshop. If this is your only reason to attend, reconsider your motivations.

The exception to this is, of course, the darkroom workshop. If you are contemplating a darkroom workshop, make sure you will have a chance to actually work. Darkroom workshops where you observe are of limited value. All your most important questions will develop as you work. If you are limited to watching, be sure you can at least call the instructor in the weeks following the workshop for telephone consultations. If they are unwilling to talk to you over the phone, go elsewhere – they only want your money.

Reason #10: See perfectly valid and sophisticated approaches and styles that may be different than your own

We are creatures of habit and nothing is so deadly to personal growth and creative art than a habit that prevents creative vision. It is a natural tendency for artists to advocate their own approach as *the approach* and *the vision*. It is good to be humbled by seeing someone's work that is both very accomplished and very different than our own. Who knows, it may open a door for you creatively.

Reason #11: Growing past the clichés

At every workshop, you will find a handful of Ansel, Brett, André, or Edward clones. This faction will clearly demonstrate the limitation inherent in blindly reproducing the *compulsories*. You will likely see four or five "Clearing Winter Storms," a few "Peppers" of various numbers, "Ship Rocks"-a-plenty, acres of "Shore Acres" (just for laughs, I have a collection of 16 prints of the very same rock from there), walls of "White House Ruins" – and an occasional truly unique and visionary body of work.

It is a fine thing to be inspired by great predecessors. Developing visual literacy and imitating our forerunners are both important learning steps. However, it is so tempting and seductive to consider this phase a destination. Attending a workshop is an effective treatment for this disease.

Reason #12: Find your own work

Once you stop imitating the Masters, it's easier to find your own imagery and purpose. The critical feedback that occurs in a workshop, the resulting introspection, and the inevitable blank wall that follows are all important parts of your progress. They may not feel like it, but they are.

Reason #13: Increase your visual literacy

Photography, like literature, has an historical backdrop. Ideally, a photographer should be familiar with the work and workers that predate him. This "visual literacy" can help one learn without "reinventing the wheel," as it were. Workshops can be very helpful in expanding one's knowledge about historical trends, fads, and movements, as well as specific images and current ideas.

Pitfalls to Avoid

Pitfall #1: Don't go to make great photographs

Long workshops are often, of necessity, scheduled during vacation time. There can be a certain pressure to make great images. You might be tempted to plan to attend a workshop so you can guarantee your vacation is filled with a certain amount of learning and artistic production. This is almost always a mistake.

If the workshop is a place to learn, it is a place to experiment. It is a place to try and fail, and then try again. It is a place to listen. It is a place to imitate. It is a place to socialize and network. There are exceptions, but unfortunately most creative photography is a lonely act. Most photographers find their best work comes when they work intensely and with great focus. This is rarely possible in the teaching atmosphere of a workshop.

Use the workshop to learn, and specifically, to learn from others. You will have the rest of your life to create great art and learn from your own experience, hopefully using some of the things learned at the workshop. If you spend your limited and valuable workshop time trying to make great images, you will likely fail to make great images and fail to learn much from the workshop opportunity.

Pitfall #2: Getting sucked into a dominant participant's

agenda

Photography is, for many, an ego-bound arena. Every workshop has at least one or two people whose primary agenda is to impress the instructor and their fellow students with their accomplishments. Their agenda does not focus on learning because they feel they have already "arrived." A look at their work is usually enough to demonstrate to everyone that they are not the masters of the craft they claim to be.

It is easy to get sucked into their need for attention – both positively and negatively. You may find their agenda fascinating and allow them to dominate the conversations. You may find their approach narrow and become angry with their selfishness. Either way, you will have allowed them to spoil your opportunity.

I've come to appreciate these people. They are searching for a "rite of passage," an institution sorely lacking in the life of the independent artist. It can be effective to quickly help this person "graduate," at that point they often turn into a workshop asset. Try talking about this "rite of passage" with them and you may find a ground for mutual understanding that will enable you to bond quickly with your fellow participants.

Pitfall #3: Field session independence

Often an enthusiasm can build during a lecture or print review session that yearns to explode when you arrive in the field. Filled with this enthusiasm, the immediate temptation is to go off in search of the great photograph. If you give in to this temptation, you eliminate one of the great reasons to attend a workshop – contact with other photographers. Again, don't waste time during the workshop doing art. You will have the rest of your life to create great works after the workshop. Instead, use your time at the workshop to observe, experiment, ask, probe, and develop contacts, friendships and resources.

Pitfall #4: Price

Be forewarned – don't underestimate the workshop's cost. From my experience, at the very least a workshop will end up costing twice the listed tuition. More often, it will cost three times that, and occasionally, four times the cost of tuition! This total cost factor includes the cost of travel, restaurant meals, film, mat board and other odds and ends you buy before going to a workshop. Yes, workshops are expensive. They are even more expensive when you are unprepared to maximize their effectiveness.

Photographers and Teachers

In the beginning of this chapter, I made some comments on the positive contribution an effective workshop instructor can make to your photographic growth. Since this is the most important element in the success of a workshop, let me add a few more comments about workshop instructors.

The main instructor, usually a "star" personality, is the principle reason most photographers choose a particular workshop. We idolize celebrities. It's fun and exciting to hang around a star for a few days and there is nothing wrong with this motivation.

There can be a big difference between a "star photographer" and someone who can help you improve your craft and imagery. Far too often, photographers are successful on the workshop circuit because of their pleasant or entertaining personality or the fine quality of their own photographs or publications – not because they are excellent teachers. Wonderful personality traits and technical expertise do not necessarily make a superb teacher. A clear distinction can be drawn between the two.

It is an old maxim that "Those that can, do. Those that can't, teach!" This phrase downplays the skills of teachers and in truth, teaching is not simple at all. Often, those that can, *do* very well, but can't *teach* worth a hoot. Teaching is a skill as complex as artmaking, and as difficult to master as photography itself. It is a rare combination to find both skills in one person. From my own experience, only 1 in 20 accomplished photographers are effective teachers.

In essence, be careful of "instructors" who are not instructors.

In my definition, a teacher is someone who helps students achieve their goals and objectives by using skillful means, compassion, wisdom, encouragement, and dedication to the student's agenda.

This is further complicated because photography is a tough way to make a living. Fine art photography is even tougher. Print sales are sporadic, produce a marginal income, and very few people can make a living selling their photographic artwork. Unfortunately, many would like to.

Among these "struggling artists" are many people who have discovered that teaching workshops provide a great meal ticket. They not only get a handsome salary for a few days of work, but their transportation is fully paid and therefore provides them the opportunity to photograph all over the country without having to pay for transportation. They also find that teaching workshops is a terrific marketing tool for selling books, posters, expensive prints, and future workshops.

In short, non-teachers generally strive to further their photographic careers and reputations. I cannot blame them for wanting to achieve these objectives. However, the proper and appropriate solitary objective for a workshop instructor should be to offer high-caliber instruction, personal contact with students, and the means for each and every one of them to further their artistic, photographic objectives, goals, and potential. All other benefits to a workshop instructor are icing on the cake and should be viewed as a bonus. These fringe benefits should not detract from providing a spirit of compassionate teaching and an attitude of service.

For example, many workshop instructors' attitudes toward field instruction appear to be, "If you want to tag along and watch how I photograph, you're welcome to do so." Although this can be an effective method of *demonstration*, it does not replace and should not dominate *instruction* – helping the student in a problem-solving, hands-on situation. Demonstration without any hands-on student participation is an ineffective approach to teaching.

In my opinion, any instructor who attends a workshop with

the objective of creating some of his own personal work during the workshop outings does not understand a workshop teacher's true objective. Workshop instructors, if they cannot resist the temptation to become absorbed in creating their own photographs, should not bring a camera into the field. They might make photographs with students in tow as a demonstration and to launch a discussion, but if the instructor leaves the students to make images on their own they are cheating the students out of the limited time and access the students have paid for.

An instructor who accepts the responsibility to serve the students understands the role of leader – that of skilled and sensitive servant.

Unfortunately, not all photographers who teach workshops are great organizers. Workshop teachers are often invited to teach because they are effective artists. True to the stereotypical image of an artist, they are often scattered and intuitive thinkers. This is a virtue in creating art, but a vice when teaching. Lack of pre-workshop preparation is one of the most consistent ways instructors fail. Specifically, they often fail to communicate with the attendees about proper preparation for the workshop.

Based on my own experiences in these situations, I've compiled the following list of items to take to a workshop that will help you maximize the workshop's benefits.

Things to Take/Prepare

Since this is a learning experience, get immediate feedback from the instructor. Polaroids or a digital camera are one of the most valuable tools you can have with you at a workshop.

Snapshots will be valuable in time. Far too often, since the workshop is perceived as a place of *art*, snapshots seem inconsequential. I have often found that reviewing snapshots has reminded me of things I was too busy to see or to fully comprehend while absorbed in a given subject. It is also interesting to photograph other people photographing, study their technique and approach the technique later via your notes and snapshots.

In good workshops, you will forge new relationships. A few weeks after the workshop is over, send a snapshot of a new friend to them along with a note of gratitude. I am amazed how many doors of long-term friendship have opened from this simple idea.

Take a tape recorder. You will need 10-20 hours of blank tape and an external microphone. Get the microphone as close to the speaker as you comfortably can. The simple truth is that effective listening also involves mental questioning, relating, organizing and brainstorming. Humans cannot possibly hear everything that is said to them in the intense environment of a workshop. Note-taking is useful but tape recording information so you can listen to it later is better. If the instructor was good and the workshop lively, listening to the discussions again via tapes will be a pleasure. (And if the instructor was bad or the group dead, you can always record over the tapes!) In addition, next month or next year, you will be at a different point in your photographic career. Re-listening to the tapes then will likely allow you to hear things that you were not prepared to hear the first time around. Common courtesy requires you to ask the instructor and the other participants if they mind if you record the event. I have often found them more than willing. As an offer of friendship, I have found it useful to make copies available to the other participants if they'd like to have their own.

Take a digital camera or E6 slide film in case there is overnight slide processing nearby. Alternatively, consider Polaroids.

Take any new books, catalogs, or other publications of interest you have that may be of interest to the others or that might stimulate conversations or ideas, e.g., Light Impressions, University Products, Calumet, Shutterbug, etc.

Other than air to breathe, coffee is the next most important survival tool for a long workshop.

Take a cushion to sit on. Hard chairs will win the battle with your derriere after about four hours.

Good workshops are on the move. You may not always be at a place where your full-sized notebook is handy. I always include both a pocket notebook and my micro tape recorder for impromptu notes in the field, cafe, car and even restroom! These can be essential to make contacts and develop relationships that last beyond the workshop. Creative ideas are not picky about when they pop into consciousness. Be prepared to capture them whenever they arrive.

After all, part of the reason you elect to attend a workshop is to place yourself in a highly charged, creative environment that will allow a great deal of both subconscious and conscious growth. If you are not prepared for this subconscious overload and the subsequent overflow of creative ideas, you run the risk of diffusing much of the workshop's benefit.

Play a game with yourself before the workshop. Imagine the workshop instructor is with you in your photographing or darkroom sessions over the weeks and months before the workshop. (Most workshops require advance registration, so you probably know far in advance that you are going to attend.)

At every opportunity, think what you would like to ask the instructor at that moment of peak activity. Jot this question down. By the time the workshop comes around, you'll have a nice list of objectives with which to begin the workshop with a running start.

This will not only focus your energies before the workshop but will also give the instructor some direction. It has been my experience that instructors often arrive with only a vague outline of the objectives and schedule for the workshop. Instructors typically begin by asking students, "What do you want to get out of this workshop?"

Every workshop instructor builds adaptability into his or her presentation to best meet the needs of the students. If you arrive with well-defined expectations, you are much more likely to influence the instructor's free time and get your objectives met.

Take negatives of particularly troublesome images. Don't just take your successes! Sure, it's nice to show off a little – everyone does it – and a workshop is a fine time and place to do so. But remember, you are attending the workshop to encourage growth, not achieve validation.

If you take field notes, bring them. If not, try to reconstruct the situations in which you took prints and negatives. Questions about these issues will surely surface, and without this information the instructor can offer little specific help.

Workshops are an ideal time to check your light meter's accuracy. During the field sessions, compare your meter's reading of a test subject to the reading someone else gets with their meter. If you do this with a dozen or so other participants, you'll get a good idea of your light meter's tendencies.

Almost without exception, workshop instructors bring work to sell at the workshop. Instructors are often artists in mid-career and their work is quite collectible. They will likely offer a substantial discount from their gallery prices.

Workshops are also a fine opportunity to buy or swap prints with your fellow students. Students are typically at the beginning of their careers and either have no gallery representation or little sales experience. If their work is of a desirable quality, you can arrange some truly outstanding bargains.

If you fail to make great art or great strides in your art career, it is always an acceptable compromise if you can just remember to have fun at a workshop.

Ten

WHEN THE FLOCK
VEERS LEFT

B ill Jay has said that he can pinpoint when a photograph
was made by comparing it with the latest trends in image
content. A photograph of a cactus was photographed with flash
in the middle of the night and, within months, cactus-flash
photographs appeared everywhere.

As the editor of *LensWork*, I can say that Bill Jay was not ex-
aggerating – in fact, he might have been quite kind. A couple of
years ago, the fad was jumping dancers caught in mid-air poses.
More recently, exactly as I had predicted, we started receiving
a number of portfolios containing portraits of naked prepubescent children – hauntingly similar to the work of Sally Mann
and Jock Sturges. In fact, this is precisely why I came out so
strongly against their work for moral and ethical reasons. It's not
that I was so much against their having done it – but rather,
I feared the Pandora's Box their work would open for the flock.

I know that by mentioning such controversial work – and then
expressing a strong opinion about it, God forbid – I run a significant risk that the real point I am hoping to make in this article
will get lost. Let me set aside the issue of photographs of naked,
prepubescent children and instead, discuss something even more
controversial – baby seals.

Some years ago, while traveling in California on business
I eked out a few days of vacation and headed for the true photog-
rapher's paradise – Point Lobos. Ben Maddow's book on Edward
Weston had recently been published and I had been eyeing those

gorgeous cliff walls, pebbly sandstone, crashing waves, dead sea life and all the other wonderful subject material that populated Point Lobos and made it some sort of photographic subject material vortex. Wanting to spend the entire day there, I headed down to Point Lobos and arrived at the entrance promptly at 6am. I was greeted by threatening signs and warnings that entry was strictly forbidden until 9am. It seems that it is impossible to gain access to Point Lobos until the baby seals have concluded their morning repast. I love baby seals as well as anyone, so I waited until 9am. I entered the park and eagerly wandered the beaches looking for those inspirational bits of landscape that Weston had made so famous. They were not there – at least I couldn't find them. At the time, I was convinced that it was a matter of light; I had been aced out of the good light by the hungry seals. If the stupid baby seals had just preferred brunch, I could have been there at the crack of dawn. I was sure that under those circumstances, I would have been able to create great artwork as Weston had done. Ah, youth is such a wonderful time for folly, wouldn't you agree?

Now that I am older and, I hope, a bit wiser, I realize that *there is absolutely nothing spectacular about Point Lobos.* Point Lobos is no different that any one of dozens of state parks or roadside attractions found in other coastal states. It's not that Point Lobos was spectacular – *it's that Edward Weston was.* Weston did not find a bit of magic landscape; it's that he was a magician in the landscape. Like so many, I had completely missed the point by assuming that Point Lobos was the place to look for photographs. The same could be said of Yosemite, Canyon de Chelley, the streets of New York City, or any one of thousands of locales that have been so beautifully photographed by the masters.

In the southeast corner of Oregon is a bit of landscape that is truly spectacular. It has the majesty of Yosemite, the Wind River Mountains in Wyoming, or Lake Louise in Glacier National Park. The Steens Mountains have Kiger Gorge, the Alvord Desert, the East Rim, Little Indian gorge, legendary wild horses, gorgeous cascading waterfalls and more wildlife than can be seen in a lifetime. So why is it that so many Oregon and Washington photographers go to Arizona to photograph the slit canyons or the Bisti Badlands, Yosemite, or Tibet?

Consider this from a different perspective. Is it just possible that Ansel Adams' photographs of Yosemite are so exceedingly well done because he *lived* there? Is it possible that Edward Weston's work on Point Lobos excels because he went there for years, in every season, every lighting condition and photographed the area again and again? I will never forget the shock I felt when I first learned that Monet, so famous for that wonderful impressionist painting of the water lily pond, had actually made a *career* of painting water lily ponds – *hundreds* of them.

There is a strange paradox at work here. On one hand, I am suggesting that copying the old masters leads to little of value. Don't go to Point Lobos because Weston had done it so well. On the other hand, I am suggesting that the masters became masters by copying themselves. The paradox is simply this: repetition of what has already been done is a useful technical exercise but rarely produces artwork of merit. Repetition of your own creative vision however, leads to refinement, increased depth and sensitivity, and generally does produce better artwork.

I will admit here that I am expressing a certain personal prejudice toward photography. I have always felt that the artist who shows us the significant in the mundane is a better artist than one who only shows us the mundane in the significant. I'll go even farther than that. I prefer the artist who shows us the significant in the mundane over the artist who shows us the significant in the significant. I prefer Weston over Adams, Josef Sudek over Eliot Porter, Paul Strand over *Time-Life*, Norman Rockwell over Picasso, Charles Dickens over James Joyce, and a good home cooked meal over *nouvelle cuisine*. Fortunately, the world of art is diverse enough that I can have my preferences and not be limited to them. (Sometimes Wagner is much more fun than Windham Hill.)

Let me conclude with some questions about Josef Sudek. When he photographed his kitchen table, his window, the little tree in his front courtyard or the egg he was about to eat for lunch, I wonder if he regretted that his circumstances prevented him from photographing in the Alps? What if he had been born in 1990s suburban America instead of 1930s Czechoslovakia? Would he have photographed shopping malls, apartment complexes, civic and bank buildings, McDonald's hamburger wrappers, and street signs? When Robert Frank, Lewis Baltz, and Robert Adams photograph such things, they always come off as somewhat sarcastic – as though the real intent of the photograph is not to show beauty, but rather to illustrate the deprivation of modern life.

You see, nostalgia is quite fashionable these days. It is easy to assume that Josef Sudek's pictures of his lunch were photographed in reverence but the reverence may only be our projection of nostalgia onto an image that had a totally different meaning for him. It's also quite fashionable to denigrate modern life. Hence, we assume that any photograph of a McDonald's hamburger wrapper is necessarily intended to express sarcastic irony.

Most artists, in spite of the myth of the isolated and tormented soul, are firmly ensconced as a part of a flock. It is just so easy to march to the beat of everybody else's drum. In contrast, the best art comes from the heart. Once technique and craft can be successfully used, the artist's real challenge begins – finding and producing from the heart. The next time the flock veers left, try turning right just for fun and leave the rest of the herd. Wander off. Look for yourself. And if you find it difficult to make a decent photograph, know you are on the correct and best path that leads to the most important artwork of your life.

Eleven

PROJECT WORK
VS. GREATEST HITS

For the last several years, I've tried to learn the methodologies and processes by which master photographers have created their great works. I've come to realize that the great works of photographic art are almost always the result of a wide-ranging *project* in which the photographer is engaged. There are lessons here for those of us creating our own artistic statements.

Project work contrasts sharply with the works of great masters as they are presented to us, the consuming public. When we see books and shows of Ansel Adams' work or that of Edward Weston, André Kertész, or Paul Strand, we are usually seeing a *greatest hits collection* of images that are each individually and independently stellar pieces of photography.

As students of the craft in beginning or mid-career, it's an easy temptation to conclude that these master photographers did their work *by searching for such stellar individual images*. It's easy to assume that at the moment of exposure the photographer heaves a sigh of relief, secure in the rush of adrenaline, aware that they had just created great art. Absolutely false. This greatest hits business is simply a myth of gigantic proportions.

These temptations and assumptions could seem unimportant and unworthy of consideration except that I *see* this assumption affecting many photographers. Their philosophy is visible in their working method – "Let's jump in the car, drive around until we see something interesting, jump out of the car, expose the negative, jump back into the car and move on to the next greatest hit."

(This has even been institutionalized as *the* method in the educational video, *Photographing with Fred Picker*.) The extension of this working method is the assumption that after enough such exposures, one has a body of work worthy of exhibition and is well on the way to developing a significant career.

This myth is very seductive, particularly when we hear apocryphal stories about the way Ansel Adams supposedly jumped out of his car and, in a matter of seconds, set up and exposed what would later become the negative that became his most famous print, *Moonrise Over Hernandez*. He was in such a hurry to create this greatest hit that, as the story goes, he didn't even have time to take a meter reading, but instead had to calculate his exposure mentally, based on his experience and knowledge of lunar luminescence.

Implied in this story is that his great success was because he was lucky enough to be at *the right place at the right time*. I confess it is a seductive myth, it implies that if *any one of us* happened to be at the right place and the right time with the right equipment and the right craft/experience that we, too, could create an historically important, creatively spectacular, and commercially successful piece of art. The challenges appear to be *having time to photograph* (which we do our best to create) and *craft*, hence our fascination with workshops that supposedly will upgrade our craft with technical insights and tricks of the trade. This myth also explains why workshops in exotic locations that allow for photographing exotic subjects are so popular.

Well, perhaps the greatest hit method does occasionally produce a fine image, just as someone does occasionally pick the correct lottery numbers!

The reality obscured by this myth is important for what it tells us about the truth of working methodologies. For example, we don't know how many times Adams drove past Hernandez, New Mexico, and looked at it under various lighting conditions, rejecting each of those moments as an unsatisfactory set of circumstances. We don't know if or how many times Adams did, in fact, photograph Hernandez only to discover later that those images failed because of some missing element. We don't know how many towns like Hernandez he photographed during his career, each time hoping for the success we see in *Moonrise*. We also don't know how many times Adams returned to photograph Hernandez again, hoping for a better image than the one we now know so well! Perhaps *Moonrise* was a one shot, photographic lottery bonanza – or perhaps the result of years of patient and repetitive work. We just don't know, well, at least I don't know. I do know that I get suspicious of success stories that imply instant success, the first time out!

I also know this: Most people aren't aware that a straight print of *Moonrise Over Hernandez* is almost unrecognizable compared to the finished print we've all seen published and reproduced so often. In the original, unmanipulated print, the sky is almost jet white and the moon is a perfect Zone X white disc in the middle of this almost-white sky. In the final print, this almost-white sky is printed to almost jet black and the moon becomes a detailed glow. One has to wonder how many test strips and practice prints it took Adams to create this final vision.

Beyond this rather simplistic example of *Moonrise Over Hernandez*, consider Edward Weston's *Pepper No. 30*. Has it occurred to you that in order for him to create the wonderful print we now know as *Pepper No. 30*, there were, previous to that, 29 versions of pepper photographs that he rejected as failures? Weston didn't create this wonderful photograph, truly one of photographic history's greatest hits, by "taking a picture of a pepper." *He made at least 30 photographs of peppers,* perhaps many more, and out of that cluster of pepper photographs, one rose to prominence as being the most significant – a greatest hit image. One could say that Weston made a *project* of photographing peppers.

Take another example, that of master photographer Paul Strand. One of the great landmark books of artistic photography is Paul Stand's *Tir a' Mhurain* – photographs of the Outer Hebrides Islands. Quite a number of the photographs from this book are routinely shown in retrospective shows and greatest hits monographs of Paul Strand's photographs. The important point is that there are many, many images in this landmark book that never make it into the retrospectives or the greatest hits catalogue. They probably are edited out of the retrospective because they are simply not as good as the others and this is as it should be. But we must be careful to note that *they were included in his original work*. His greatest hits were originally produced in the context of the project of images, published in his book.

Strand didn't set out to make a greatest hit; he set out to make a book containing lots of fine photographs. His *project* was photographing the Hebrides Islands and publishing this book. But to a large degree Strand's *legacy* (as defined by his retrospectives in the greatest hits publications) are only a few of the images that he thought were good enough to include in this book project.

The same can be said of Weston's seminal book, *California and the West*. This book, published in 1940, contained 92 photographs – one of which is his now famous *Zabriskie Point, Death Valley*. The book contains several other prints you and I probably would not have printed, let alone have published!

A more contemporary example is Robert Adams. Adams has published no fewer than seven project-oriented books, but is best known for half a dozen images that have been published in book reviews, retrospectives, group exhibitions and group publications. He even contributes to this greatest hits mentality with the publication of his recent book, *To Make It Home; Photographs of the American West*.

I don't fault this editorialism that creates retrospective greatest hits. In fact, I applaud it – the best does rise and survive. I do think however, that it's erroneous for working photographers to assume that master photographers set out to create greatest hit images or even that they recognized them as greatest hits during or shortly after completing their projects. Instead, I suspect, the master photographers focused their energies on the projects and the broad spectrum of photographs they were including in those projects. In each and every case, they made the best photographs possible with their vision, capabilities, and talents.

It was only later, and almost incidentally, that time, the public, and the selective hands of editors separated some of those images from the project work.

It's interesting to note that André Kertész produced a series of celebrity portraits for publication in the serial article that occurred each month in the United Airlines in-flight magazine, *Vis à Vis*. As a frequent traveler, I've come to appreciate the portraits featured. I'm sure that a few of these will survive the test of time and be reproduced for future generations in his greatest hits monographs as significant pieces of work. I'm equally sure that the vast majority of them will not. The point is not that some of these are great photographs and some of them are not – it is his *project methodology* that is of interest. He just continued producing the work – the great, the good, the bad, and the ugly – and let time take its course.

It behooves us as working artists to recognize the power of this project-oriented mentality. Define a project and work with intensity and discipline to produce a large number of images. Then edit to a finite, final selection. To repeatedly approach the same subject over and over again, as Weston did with his peppers, is a method more likely to produce significant results than random image-making in search of the elusive greatest hit.

Project photography does have its risks – a project may fail – but it's not necessary that every image or every project be a rousing success. The *process* and *progress* are more important than any single image or result. I cringe when I hear people say a photographer's career is washed-up because his latest project was critically derided. When working in project methodologies, you must recognize that some images are going to shine and some are not; some are going to live and some are not; some projects will be successful and some will not. I applaud every time a photographer completes a body of work even if some are more successful than others.

Please don't misunderstand me here. I do not suggest you should accept mediocre images as part of your personal project. I fully believe that every image in Strand's book was photographed, printed, and selected for the book because Strand thought it was the absolute winner of the publication – every image, every time. If he didn't have that kind of faith in an image, he would likely have excluded it from the publication. This is a matter of personal integrity.

I also cringe when I hear a photographer tell me that he or she is not interested in traveling to location XYZ to photograph because they have already photographed there once before. *Because they have already photographed there?!* What about changing seasons? What about changing light? What about natural erosion? What about the changes wrought by humanity? What about the passage of time, the aging of people and the changing of cultures? What about – and this might be the most important changing element of all – the changing sensibilities, sensitivities, and creative vision of the photographer?

I've been to the Foree Fossil Beds near John Day, Oregon, to photograph no less than 24 times. I made an exceptional image on trip number 3 and trip number 18, and good images on four other occasions. All these trips might appear to be a waste of time, but in my estimation they are not. If I hadn't gone the second time, I couldn't have gone a third, fourth, eighteenth, or twenty-third time. Is it merely a coincidence that Adams spent a lifetime photographing in Yosemite and is famous and known for those images? Is it a coincidence that Weston spent a lifetime photographing on Point Lobos and that many of these are his most well-known images? Repetition is a recurring theme in project photography.

I wonder how many negatives Adams and Weston exposed, developed, and printed that we *never* see but that exist in their archives as "failures." One of my favorite quotes from Ansel Adams is that "One has to make 10,000 negatives before one is really a photographer." What he didn't say, but I suspect he intended, was that a whole lot of those negatives have to be of the same subject in the same place, doing them over and over and over again, learning and improving as one progresses.

When I was teaching photography in the 1970s, I challenged

my students to make 100 finished prints of a chosen subject or theme. Even if the project is burned upon completion, the *process* is invaluable for growth and for learning the virtues of the project-oriented approach. I'll guarantee that out of 100 finished prints of a *project*, there will be a few that are truly outstanding greatest hits. Alternatively, make 100 random photographs of random subjects. I'll bet a fair number won't even be memorable and a considerable number will simply look like other photographers' greatest hits. Only by working through the "compulsories" can you begin to see your own imagery. This reason alone might be reason enough to try a defined-project approach.

Process is, in my opinion, the essence of project photography. It seems grossly arrogant to assume that you can make a great image, *your best image*, of a subject the first time. Project-oriented photography is a commitment to process and to growth. It creates a collection of hundreds of negatives and dozens of images of the defined project.

Have you ever taken a still life photograph of a flower? You may have this image in your portfolio of greatest hits. If so, I'd like to encourage you to take a look at a book called *Hana* (Japanese for flower) by Japanese photographer Yasuhiro Ishimoto. This book contains 128 black and white still life photographs of flowers. When I first heard about this book, I assumed it would be repetitious and boring. It is not. Ishimoto's example of project-oriented photography is an inspiration and classic lesson. It demonstrates how dedication to making a hundred images of a defined theme will help/force/motivate you to think more deeply, creatively, and innovatively about something as simple as a black and white photograph of a flower.

Indeed, if you cannot make 100 images of a project theme, it is likely that you are not looking very creatively at the subject. Part of the project approach is the frustrating wall of self-limitations that you must work through after making the *easy* images. This is no fun and, therefore, feels like it should be avoided. If photography is a hobby, it *can* be avoided. If you want to make significant art, however, growing beyond the "easy ones" is the entire purpose of your work. Arriving at the wall of limitation is not a dead end; it's the beginning of your real career, the artist's moment of truth.

This is the *koan* of photography. Photography is an instant process, accessible to the masses. It requires only a little experience and some affordable equipment. It seems as though it should be easy. Pop out of the car and make great art. Easy, but it is not. It is seductive and frustrating. It is demanding and unforgiving. It is only accessible through great effort, dedication, repetition and hard work. To think otherwise is a fool's dream. Accept all the lucky ones the cosmos throws your way, but luck is a shaky foundation on which to build a career.

Twelve

IMAGE & IDEA

I once met Ansel Adams at a gallery opening where I shook his hand. It was a Walter Mitty moment. For those of you who don't remember Walter Mitty, he's the fictional character who constantly lived a life of fantasy where he was the hero, the daring pilot, the celebrity, or the spy. In reality, he was just an average Joe who dreamed of someday being somebody. Shaking Ansel Adams' hand was, for me, a Walter Mitty moment. I was ready to receive some sort of magical transference of cosmic photographic wonderstuff. I fully expected that my photographs would suddenly become better. It didn't happen.

Instead, I became an *ARAT* photographer – a term a friend uses (somewhat disparagingly) for "Another Rock, Another Tree." The question is: who cares about these images? I ask this question seriously. *Who cares* that I've made another photograph of a compositionally interesting rock, tree, riverbed, sand dune, or (you fill in the blank). Like so many photographers I know, after pursuing these kinds of images for years, I eventually had to look back and assess the results. Years of productive energy had generated a body of work that was nothing more than Another Rock, Another Tree. Boring photographs, done so much better by so many others so many times before me. This is not to say there is inherently anything wrong with photographing rocks and trees. Rocks and trees are not the problem, nor is landscape photography in general. The problem lies not with the subject material but with the *content*. To put it bluntly, the problem lies with the *photographer.*

Let me back up, stop talking about photography and talk instead, about Art. (Yes, the sarcasm is fully intended.) Although I'm fully committed to photography as my personal art medium, I find that more and more I'm drawn to learning about the history of painting, sculpture and other traditional art mediums. (As an aside, isn't it strange that I need to offer this mild apology in a chapter written specifically for photographers? Why is it that the history of photography is not more integrated and intertwined with the history of traditional art?)

One of the key ideas that surface constantly in the history of art is that great paintings, sculptures, and music are usually tied to a set of ideas that can be verbalized, if not by the artist, then at least by others. This is represented clearest in religious iconography, of course. Every painting from the early Christian era to the beginning of the Renaissance has some iconographic purpose; usually, to simply illustrate a bible story or moment. The idea in the painting is the idea within the story. In fact, one of the problems in looking at these paintings in the 21st century is that so many of us don't understand the stories contained in the imagery. Without a grasp of biblical history, characters, parables, or even liturgy, so many of these religious paintings are undecipherable to the average person. In fact, almost without exception, the first key to understanding painting prior to the Renaissance is to develop an understanding of the mythology represented. Study any art history book and you'll find that much of it is acquainting today's readers with the stories in the paintings. Yet, these stories were universally understood by the patrons and viewers when the paintings were created.

To illustrate this point (in a slightly silly way), I need only ask you what comes to mind when you hear the phrase "Gilligan, little buddy"? With no more explanation than those three words, the vast majority of Americans will understand the reference instantly. To an audience in another time or place who are denied the sophisticated culture of the 1960s TV sitcom, *Gilli-*

gan's Island, the phrase would be meaningless, or at least require a thorough explanation. (Wouldn't *that* be fun to watch!) Often, these cultural references are so subtle and so assumed that we, who understand them automatically, find the need for explanations amazing.

The more I studied art, the more obvious the need for greater understanding became. I developed an interest in Japanese woodblock prints – an art form know as *ukiyo-e*. These prints often depict *instances* – almost photographic in their desire to capture *time* – that show us a peak moment in a tale from Japan's rich mythology. These can convey the subtle facial expression of a Kabuki actor, a portrait of a famous military general reflecting on fate a moment before an important battle, or a thousand other images that are undecipherable unless you are thoroughly knowledgeable about Japanese history and mythology. Without this background, my first task in understanding each print is to first become acquainted with the story behind it. Only then can I appreciate the talent that the artist used in bringing out this image.

The key idea here is that *art is about ideas*. As photographers – as graphic artists – it may be easy to dismiss this concept and to insist that photographs should be seen as idea-less graphics. The proposition that a photograph has to contain a story or represent a philosophy might seem absurd. I've heard this prejudice defended by comparing fine art photographs to impressionist paintings, for example, as a means of justifying that photographs are suppose to be just shapes, tones and forms. This sounds justifiable until you study the history of impressionism and come to understand the ideas behind the impressionist movement. Impressionist painters were reacting against the literal realism of their predecessors. That is to say, the *idea* behind impressionism is that a painting *could* be simply color and texture and juxtaposition. Without taking the time to provide ultimate proof within each art movement, I'll propose the bold, universal statement that *all great artwork is about a preceding and underlying idea* and this idea is what gives *meaning* and, more importantly, *importance* to the artwork. It is this meaning that facilitates the connection between the audience and the artwork. If a picture is more than just a picture, it must relate to the viewer. This relationship is often defined by the idea within the work of art.

But is this true in photography? In particular, is this true in *fine art* photography? I have thought about this and I've concluded that it is. It didn't even take much analysis to come to this conclusion. Try the following experiment: List as many great photographs you can – for example: *Clearing Winter Storm, Moonrise Over Hernandez, Pepper No. 30, Navigation Without Numbers* (to name a few of my personal favorites!) – make the list as long as you like. Now see if you can find any images in your list that *don't* have some idea that can easily be associated with them.

Since I started this article with him, I'll use Ansel Adams' great work to construct an example. Consider the body of work from his book *Yosemite: Range Of Light*. What is the *idea* behind this body of work? Quite simply, Adams' work in the pristine landscape is about the *pristine* landscape. I believe Ansel Adams became the most famous photographer in our times because his images of the pristine landscape mirrored the philosophy of the American environmental movement just as it was gaining momentum and a large, enthusiastic following. His images reflect the sanctity of the natural environment and the beauty of unspoiled nature. Rather than seeing Adams in context with his peers in photography, consider his philosophical peers. He is *not* a fellow traveler of photographers like Walker Evans or Henri Cartier-Bresson, at least not if you compare the content of their imagery. In content, he is a fellow traveler of outdoorsmen John Muir, John Burroughs, and Henry David Thoreau. Their ideas about nature and mankind's place in nature are visible in Adams' photographs. His images do not merely *illustrate* their ideas but *embody, reflect and visualize* their concepts.

Photographs – at least good ones – are always about *ideas*; without ideas photographs are merely images. For an image to be idea-less is as emasculating as a paragraph without a thought. It is as easy to make a photograph without content as it is to write a sentence that doesn't say anything. Both are common, both are prevalent, and both are useless. This is not to say that photographs are mere illustrations, nor does this subjugate photography to philosophy. I am not demeaning photography with this assertion; I am trying to illustrate a principle that can be useful for photographers. What are the ideas, assumptions, stories, thoughts that offer meaning to your images?

As a test of this theory, consider the images that would result from a totally random series of exposures. Imagine a roll of film with 36 images of whatever happened to be in front of you at random periods of time. Imagine that these images are shot without composition, without forethought, without trying to make an interesting photograph. If it were possible to make interesting photographs this way we would. In fact, Garry Winogrand tried this, but found that not every image was significant. Some were, but the interesting images were those that happened, by sheer coincidence, to bring meaning and an idea into the visual graphic. In fact, his whole approach was to allow the meaningful into his images in a totally random and unpremeditated way. That, in itself, is *an idea that lies behind* his photography.

Part of the reason I think this discussion is so important is that it has practical consequences for the act of photographing. If one is to photograph on purpose, with the intent of recording or embodying an idea in a photograph, then *why* one photographs and *what* one photographs is influenced by the ideas that precede it. (For those who prefer to keep the process of *photographing* more fluid and less restricted, then the idea is post-meditated and therefore, comes *after photographing* but *before printing*. In this case, the idea-inclusive act is one that takes place in the darkroom, rather than in the field.) I was photographing with a friend not long ago and asked him "What are you interested in photographing today?" He responded "Oh, I don't care, just anything!" But, in fact, this wasn't true at all or we wouldn't have needed to go out *seeking* photographic subjects. He could have just randomly aimed, Winogrand-style. *"But that's not photography!"*

Then you must have an *idea* about what is and what isn't worth photographing!

I've asked myself many times, "What to photograph?" Yet, this is the wrong question. What I really needed was not an interesting photographic *subject* but an *idea* – the most elusive element in all artmaking.

If ideas do not lie at the center of a work of art, then art can just as easily be made by a monkey or a machine. I've heard that Morley Baer used to say that in order to be a good photographer you must first be a good person. By that, I don't think he simply meant a *moral* person or a *righteous* person, but more that you need to be an *interesting* person, a person with depth, maturity, wisdom and vision. In order to use a camera to say something, you must first have something to say or the resulting photographs will be meaningless and powerless.

This is not to say, however, that photographs are mere illustrations of ideas. They are not superfluous to the verbally expressed idea. In fact, images – like music – can be a more powerful way of expressing ideas *because* they are non-verbal. Verbal expressions have the obvious disadvantages of requiring a common language and a common understanding of the subtle nuances possible with language. Artistic imagery and music side-step these difficulties by focusing on the non-verbal aspect of communication. But, just as words are symbols for things, so images have symbols that need to be understood.

This business of symbols and meaning is one of the more complex challenges for artists, especially today. The world is so complex and civilization has developed a rich and varied accumulated body of thought. We can easily lose sight of the fact that the symbols we use in our artwork will entirely fail to communicate without presumptive understanding. For example, as I drive, I occasionally see symbols on a bumper sticker or the fender of a car – the outline of a fish, a sequence of colors imitating a rainbow, a donkey, an elephant, or a U.S. or foreign flag – to name just a few. Each of these symbols *means* something and communicates something about the occupant's beliefs or life.

Have you ever seen a symbol on a bumper sticker and had no idea what it symbolized? This is precisely the feeling of illiteracy I had when I visited Japan and found myself surrounded by billboards with Japanese characters. It is precisely what happens when photographers present images to a public who is uneducated in the symbolism of our culture or the symbolism of photography. You will see my photograph of a pepper and place it in context with the history of photographed peppers. (We know there were at least thirty of them!) It's easy to mistakenly assume that other people – that is, non-photographers – can see in our photographs what we see without the benefit of our photographic education and visual literacy. Inside jokes can be fun, but they can just as easily alienate the audience if the references are unknown. Our indiscriminant use of symbols can obfuscate the ideas and the meaning in our images.

Here is a classic lesson from history. There was a time in ancient Japan in which the poets of the day made poems that referenced other great poets. In order to understand their poetry, you needed to understand their inferences and references. In turn, poets then used these poems and references as second generation references. Complexity grew upon complexity until eventually only the poet literati could understand Japanese poetry, and poetry degenerated into a game of who could "out-reference" whom. For the participants, it was great fun, but for everyone else it became meaningless and tortured. In opposition to this trend Basho began writing his simple, straight-forward, unambiguous *haiku*. He reinvented Japanese poetry and turned the entire focus on experience itself. As a result, his poetry could be understood and appreciated by everyone – even illiterate peasants – and has survived for five hundred years.

There is a delicate balance between imagery that contains *no* idea and imagery that contains too many subtle symbols, subtle layers of meaning, and circular references. It is easy to burden a photograph with ideas or symbols that make it illegible. It is easy to make a photograph that is merely *zones and tones*. I suggest avoiding both extremes. The photograph with no idea behind it fails to capture the imagination, fails to motivate, fails to engage, and is ultimately lifeless. The photograph with too much symbolism or that makes a conscious attempt to embody too many ideas and contemporary philosophies is equally lifeless. Finding this balance is one of the challenges to making art that has value and meaning to other people – that speaks to an audience.

So where does this leave photography that has no underlying idea, photography that is tones without a spirit? It seems to me that a photographer who takes such images is exactly like a pianist who repeatedly plays the scales. These are important exercises to develop your skills and technical abilities and are not to be overlooked – nor overvalued. The pianist who plays notes without feeling is not an artist. Neither is the photographer who presents zone-and-tone without passion. Passion is emotion, involvement, connection, and these are the result of an idea. As David Hurn has said in *On Being a Photographer*, "photograph what you are interested in." That you are interested in something means that it captures your imagination, and *that* implies there is an idea you find fascinating. Let that idea be the beginning of your creative efforts. If your work is done well, your passion for that idea will translate into the photographs and this will pique the viewer's curiosity, too. Once you have their interest, your photographs will be engaging and your ideas will come through.

Thirteen

THE IMPORTANCE
OF PARTNERING

Photography tends to be a solitary activity. Of course, it's not necessary, but it often becomes so, particularly for the fine art photographer. Photographing is usually a slow, methodical, non-spectator sport. It's truly one of the best tests of spousal fidelity: if you doubt this, take your spouse with you the next time you head out with your 8x10 camera into the grand landscape. Likewise, darkroom work is also often solitary. Most photographers prefer to develop their own film, make their own prints, and even cut their own matboards and frame the photographs themselves. Some assistance is acceptable, particularly if they're paid employees or apprentices, but, somehow, sending work to a lab feels just a bit like cheating or perhaps a bit too commercial.

Photography courts the cult of the rugged individualist, the solitary artist, the photographer who mixes their own chemistry and spends the vast majority of their life with brown-stained fingernails. It is the image we have of Edward Weston and Ansel Adams standing alone in the grand landscape, heads cocked high, peering down at the f/stop numbers on their view camera lenses, perched on the edge of some precipice overlooking a landscape of incomparable beauty. It is a seductive image. It is, far too often, a myth that can lead you astray. The truth is that most photographers will find themselves more productive, more creative, more effective, and better photographers if they can recognize the importance of partnering.

Partnering with other artists

Let me ask this question: Do you remember the movie *Dances with Wolves*? Who's movie was that? Movie fans and those with good memories will immediately say, "It was Kevin Costner's movie." Was it *just* Kevin Costner's movie? He partnered with literally hundreds of people. There were financiers, actors, production assistants, sound engineers, caterers, costume designers, promotion and marketing people, historians, landowners, and the list goes on. But, *who's movie was it?* It was Kevin Costner's movie! And we say so because it was Kevin Costner's *vision*, Kevin Costner's *will*, and Kevin Costner's *leadership* that brought this artistic idea into tangible form for all of us see.

So why can't the same partnering be applied in fine art photography? Commercial photographers recognize this advantage and partner every day. Art directors, assistants, lighting specialists, photo labs, equipment rental businesses, and location and set designers are often a part of commercial photographic assignments. So why is it that fine art photographers almost always insist on working alone? Is it necessary, or is it *a habit*?

While interviewing Huntington Witherill about his *Botanical Series*, the question of partnering came up. His *Botanicals Series* includes still life photographs of dried, pressed flowers arranged carefully on backdrops that were oil paintings, watercolors, or parts thereof. He told me that he began this project by making contact with a woman whose business was providing dried, pressed flowers. He discussed his photographic idea with her and developed a partnership (i. e., an exchange of flowers for photographs) that used her expertise in growing, gathering, and pressing flowers that made beautiful photogenic objects. He also partnered with a painter who provided backdrops of watercolor paintings and oil paintings which he used in his still life arrangements. Eventually, he even partnered with us to publish these images in *LensWork*. It was his openness to partnering that made this project easier and more available to a wider audience.

His comments led me to an exercise with a photographic project that I was just beginning. I asked myself an interesting series of questions: Who could help me with this? Why would they be interested in helping me with this? Whose expertise might be useful? What am I missing that would make this project easier? Where do I find the answers I need? How do I gain the cooperation of others? What aspects of the project am I willing to give up to more successfully achieve the ultimate end?

The more I thought about this idea of partnering, the more I realize that it was not only a key to success, but *had been* the key to success on all the projects I'd ever done that had become visible, meaningful, important, and were not stuck either in my head or on the top shelf of my storage closet.

During an interview, David Grant Best posed a related question that he finds useful in his work. He often asks himself, "How far can I take this game?" He tends to think of everything he does as a game – not in the trivial sense, not in the competitive sense, but in the *playful* sense. The minute you ask "How far can I take this game?" it begs the second question, "How far can I take it if I get someone else involved?" My dad used to say that "two heads were better than one, even if one of them was a cabbage head." If you want to fully explore an idea, it might not be best to work in a vacuum. It seems perfectly reasonable that two or three people collectively might have more creative ideas than one person working alone.

Partnering with other ideas

There is one other idea that comes into play in this line of thought. This idea comes from unexpected quarters – *comedy theory*. I remember once hearing a comedian explain that the fundamental basis for comedy is to break an expected pattern of events. 1) Establish the premise for the sequence; 2) Move the audience along an expected direction; and finally, C) Trip them up with something unexpected! The humor is in the unexpected.

In an related way, the same idea can be used in creative photography – at least the idea of the *unanticipated thought pattern*. One of the most interesting ways to create new ideas is to *combine things that don't look like they should go together*. What do you get if you cross a used car salesman with a post-modernist? It sounds like a joke (and in fact is a funny one) but it's also a useful exercise in creativity. Taking two such disparate objects and thinking about how they can combine in unexpected ways can be a creative exercise that leads to some fascinating new ideas – ideas that may remain hidden unless such an exercise in partnering is employed.

Each one of us has a variety of experiences that make up our accumulated memory of life. We have knowledge of a variety of different places, sports, cooking, business, travel, education, literature – an almost endless list. What happens if elements from one area of your life sneak over and become useful in another area? What if you mix your interest in sports with your interest in cooking and again with your interest in photography? (I suppose you could photograph a food fight!) This partnering of ideas can be used in simple thought-experiments to ask "What if …?" or perhaps in more tangible projects engaged with enthusiasm. It's often been said that there are no new ideas, there are just new ways to *use* the old ideas. Just as when partnering with other people, a partnering of ideas can be just as unpredictably productive. The key idea here is ECRS – Eliminate, Combine, Rearrange, and Simplify. I first heard this formula thirty years ago in a business seminar and I find it just as instructive today when thinking about artwork.

The punchline is, by the way, "An offer you can't understand!"

Fourteen

Windows & Artifacts

A while back, I found myself staring at a photograph hanging on the wall in my doctor's office. It was like a thousand other images we've all seen in such situations – a beautiful color photograph of nature's splendor depicting something or other. Of course, waiting for the doctor is a high stress moment, filled with anxiety. It's probably not uncommon in such situations for patients to seek comfort wherever possible. I was easing my stress by looking at this photograph. Yet, my reactions to it were more unusual and specific than the average viewer, I'm sure.

As a photographer, I usually look at photographs differently and more intently than I would if I were not involved in the photographic arts. So, I was surprised when I found myself looking at this image on my doctor's wall not as a piece of photography at all. Instead, I was staring right *through* the photographic emulsion. I was engaged in a fantasy. I was pretending, on a very subconscious level, that I was looking at the beautiful scene itself *as though it were a scene outside a window*, the window being defined by the photograph's frame. In my fantasy experience, the photograph didn't exist at all. This is a subtle fantasy and one worth examining for its impact on us photographers.

My experience with this photograph contained a set of assumptions of which I was unaware until I thought about them more deeply.

1.   I pretended that the doctor's office happened, by sheer

coincidence, to be constructed in a location that allowed the architect to include this window in the construction plans.

2.   I pretended that this window just happened to overlook a gorgeous view of a pristine mountain peak from a perfect, pristine lake.

3.   Furthermore, the fantasy assumed that nature had frozen the lighting conditions so that the eternal sunset vision, through this window, was continually seen through crisp, clear air with beautiful, golden sunlight glinting off the pristine lake and the snowy mountain top.

I must admit, I sat there for a few minutes absorbed in the simple act of escape and enjoyment of this vision through the doctor's office window. As a waiting patient, I was glad that the image had been photographed, produced, sold, and hung right there for my use at that moment.

The reason to focus on this expericence in this article is: I had not enjoyed the photograph, but I *had* enjoyed *the fantasy of viewing the subject matter.* There is a very fine but significant distinction between these two experiences. As I've reviewed this idea over the last several months, I've come to realize the importance of this difference for working photographers and its impact on our product, marketing, and, to a large degree, our collective frustration in selling photographic works.

Let me be as precise as possible. The difference I am attempting to describe is the difference between *the photograph as a window* and *the photograph as an artifact.* I believe this ability for a photograph to be misconstrued *as a window* is one of the chief oddities that makes photographic art unique in the art world.

To clarify this point, I will artificially and simplistically dissect the experience of viewing art. When a sculptor, a potter, or a painter (with the exception of the photographic realist movement), a fiber artist, or even a performing artist, creates art, *the audience is not supposed to look past the art or through the art at some "real" subject behind or beyond the artist's product itself.* We direct our attention to the art product itself – the art-ifact, as it were. In a museum or gallery, we look at a sculpture as an *artifact.* We look *at* the sculpture. We look *to* it. We focus *on* it. We are involved in its *surface, shape* and *form.* For clarification, I'll call this the *primary perceptive experience.*

We try to assimilate the sculpture into our consciousness and, from that perceptive experience, we derive (create?) a feeling, an emotion, a response. I'll call this created experience the *secondary emotional experience.*

The painting, sculpture or pottery is the basis for a primary perceptive experience and, as such, it is the foundation on which the secondary emotional experience is generated. Photography deviates from this traditional experience. When I viewed the photograph in the doctor's office, the photograph was not the basis for the perceptive experience – *the mountain scene itself was.* The mountain scene was the artifact that created, in turn, the secondary emotional experience of easing my stress. In this case, the photograph served as mere *mechanical media.*

This, it occurs to me, can be a great weakness with photographic art. When a photograph functions as a window, as mechanical media, it is not looked *at*, it is looked *through*. It is not an artifact; it is a transparency. It's viewed as though it literally does not exist, and through it the viewer is transported through time and space to a moment and a location where he can directly view the subject matter.

Whereas the experiential focus of the sculpture, the teapot, the collage, or the performance is *the here* and *the now*, the experiential focus of the photograph is *the there* and *the then*. The best photograph is the one that does this transportation fantasy the most successfully. So all the tourists from Iowa and Kansas, when they're lucky enough to have the opportunity to vacation in Yosemite, can stand on Wawona Point and exclaim without irony and without inconsistency, "Oh dear, doesn't it look just like a picture," and then jerk their 35mm camera to their eye and snap a tourist photograph.

Inherent in their action is the assumption that the creation of a good photograph takes little or no skill or talent whatsoever, but merely the good fortune to be *there*, *then*. It assumes the glass of the camera lens is a window and like all windows, there is no talent necessary to use it effectively. Anyone with natural human sight can make the photograph. The assumption is that photography is not dependent on *vision, craft, sensitivity, courage, dedication*, or *raw talent*. The assumption is essentially that photography is nothing more than the good fortune to have time to travel and money for photographic equipment. So the tourist says, "Five hundred dollars for a picture? Shoot, I coulda done that for nothin'!"

Some photographers understood this dilemma and tried to overcome this limitation of the window by turning their photographs more directly into artifacts. I suspect this is one of the primary motivations behind the hand-colored image – a technique that places the final product precariously in between a straight photograph and a painting. The very application of pen, pencil, brush, or charcoal to the surface of a photograph suddenly turns it into an object, an artifact. This is even more true with a photograph by a very famous and well-known photographer. With an Ansel Adams or an Edward Weston signature, an image will sell for a much higher price than a hand-colored one by an unknown, contemporary artist. My proposal is that the Ansel Adams or the Edward Weston photograph has also been manipulated by the pen – the artist's signature turns the photograph into an artifact.

By the way, I believe this "window" business is precisely why photographic books sell so well. Most of us who buy photographic books do so *rather than buy photographic prints*. On the surface, this looks as though it may be strictly a price consideration. Obviously, a few dozen photographs would cost many times the price of the same number of images cost in the form of a photographic book.

The images we buy in book form, particularly with the newer technologies of laser scanning, duo-tone and tri-tone image printing, make the images in today's photography books very closely approximate the real photographs. The technologies do this so well that many of us feel when we buy the book that *we have purchased something that is as good as the real photograph*, that is to say, good enough to allow us *to clearly view the subject*. The book's ability to transport us to a direct viewing of the subject is good enough to make the purchase of the original artwork unnecessary. Again, the assumption in this thought is that the photograph itself is not an artifact, but merely a window to a time and place. If the book is an equally good window, why waste money on an original print?

Fifteen

Quod Erat Faciendum

"It is Finished"

Picasso advised that the most valuable lesson a painter could learn was in knowing when to stop. In the case of photographers, stopping is not the issue – the shutter takes care of that in jig time. Based on my own experience, *finishing* is the lesson of challenge for photographers.

When Picasso died, he supposedly left 90,000 complete pieces of artwork. Humph! We photographers know this is nothing! Garry Winogrand left 10,000 rolls of undeveloped film. This situation illustrates the problem perfectly. The curse of photography is that it is so easily confused with *photographing* – the confusion of verb and noun. Photography takes form in finished edition prints, books, posters, exhibitions, and most commonly individually matted and framed original photographs. To be blunt, if you "take pictures," you are not yet a photographer. It is only when you *finish them* that you qualify for the moniker, and finishing requires the C-word – *commitment*. Someone once humorously observed that if you buy a camera you're a photographer, but if you buy a piano, you own a piano. What makes this line funny is that we know it is both simultaneously true and not true at the same time. Taking pictures and banging on the piano are both possible and fun, but these do not make you a photographer or a pianist.

By this I don't mean the commitment of disciplined working; I mean the commitment of saying in precise photographic qualities exactly what you mean to say, unambiguously and with finality. There are two trends in photography that I detest; purposeful ambiguity held up as a virtue and so-called *"objective photography,"* where the image-maker is supposed to be transparent and *non sequitur* to the result. The first is so non-committal that it is essentially empty; the second so lacks ideas that it is meaningless. There is no more naked admittance than when a photographer shows work that is still a verb – "This isn't finished yet – a work still in progress – a work print – *I have no idea what I am doing here but by showing a work of potential perhaps I can steal from you an idea worthy of completion.*"

When you make a photograph and finish it, you make a tacit statement　– "I think this is so important, so meaningful, so worthy of your attention that I am presenting it to you with all this fanfare." If it is important, it deserves finishing. If it is not, it does not. This seems so simple in theory, but is so difficult in practice. It's easier to just leave the work unfinished – in a perpetual state of *potential.* The subtle delusion here is "If I *never* finish the work, it will remain a work of *potential genius.* If I finish it, it will demonstrate in unambiguous terms that it is a work of banality." I understand this fear because I am often stuck in the same rut myself. As a result, I've developed a specific strategy to deal with the problem of incomplete work, and that strategy is the subject of this article.

First, let me offer an explanation that *is* valid for at least some photographers. Quite simply, printing is a dismal disappointment. On the other hand, photographing is so full of potential, so full of life, so replete with brilliance, genius and creative vision unparalleled in the history of the medium. After the euphoria of photographing, you develop the negatives. What was brilliant now appears very, very good. Then you make the contact sheets. What was very, very good is now good. Then you make the first proof enlargement. What was good is suddenly crap; you question your career; you feel you are worthless dog meat with no talent, no vision, no hope whatsoever of financial success or fame.

In short, if printing is such a failure and photographing is such a success why not just stop at the phase of photographing and feel so much better about yourself?

Worse, printing does not end the pain. Because, just like in golf, there is an occasional flash of brilliance – a print that works, an image that keeps you picking up the camera and shooting more film. If it wasn't for that one decent golf shot in the round or that one nice image in the shooting session, I'm sure golfers and photographers would even *more* readily turn to alcohol.

So a terrific image has been printed and now it is time to tone it, mat it, spot it, frame it, hang it on the wall, and show all your friends, patrons, and strangers who visit the gallery that represents you. Then, on the opening night, you overhear (because you are straining so hard to do so) the comments that people make about your work. "It's too bad he can't afford color film. This one would have been nice in color." "I once did a shot just like that on vacation." "That's such a great photograph! I think I will do one just like it on my next vacation." "I love the mat board." "I wonder what f/stop he used?" "They had an exhibition here last year with a guy who did the same kind of images, but his were better."

This is the harvest of finishing. It's no wonder so many photographers don't.

Don't be too discouraged. There is actually some good news at the end of this rather bleak tunnel. I first got a glimpse of this when I attended an Owens Valley Photography workshop taught by Bruce Barnbaum, John Sexton and Ray McSavaney. Each of the three instructors took a third of the group aside for individual one-on-one critiques. During the course of the week-long workshop, we had an opportunity to have our work critiqued independently by each of the three instructors. My first critique was by Bruce Barnbaum. He is a tough critic with the appropriately high standards of a great teacher. He lined up all my photographs and then set aside four he really liked. Then he started telling me how terrible most of them were – he didn't like this one, he didn't like that one, he didn't like this one either, but that one had some potential, here was one he thought was just horrible. The critique went on for six or seven years; it felt like it, anyway. The next day, in the John Sexton group, I was so intimidated I waited to go last and only then after John prodded me relentlessly. I put up the same images, in the same order, and waited for John's criticism to deepen my depression. He looked for a long time and then started in. "I like this one, I really like this one, this one's very close and just needs a little extra printing in the corner, this doesn't strike me but it's just because I can't relate to the subject material, this one I would scrap, but all in all I would say your portfolio is good." I was astonished, a bit numbed. The next day, I was in the Ray McSavaney group. Ray liked all the ones that John and Bruce didn't, didn't like the ones that Bruce did, and made no comments about the rest.

I had learned a valuable lesson. Show your work to a hundred different people and you will get a hundred different opinions, none of them correct *and all of them valid.* All their opinions are valid because when someone tells you whether or not they like your work, there is no way to argue with that – to do so would only question their taste, not evaluate your work.

To put it another way, in the real world, there is no such work as good work and bad work. There is only work that you finish and work you do not. Don't finish any work, no one will find any fault with it. If you finish work, some people will find fault with it. These are immutable axioms. When you think about it, there is only one intelligent strategy; do your work and let the chips fall where they may. There are, however, a couple of strategies that can be useful.

Let Go

How can you complete your second portfolio until you have completed your first? You cannot do your hundredth finished print until you have done your tenth, your fiftieth, and your ninety-ninth. I'm convinced that a person can only have a limited number of projects and creative ideas at one time. For example, if you can have fifteen good, creative photographic ideas in your mind at one time, then doesn't it make sense that you can't think of your sixteenth idea until you let go of one of the first fifteen and can make mental room for the next creative idea? The best way to do new work, to be motivated, is to complete the old work so that you can let go of it. We all know someone who has been nursing the same project for *years* and is no closer to finishing it now than when you first met them? As the old maxim says, "When you stay in the same rut long enough, it begins to feel normal."

Deadlines

Whether you are in business, art, painting, gardening, or even photography, objectives are only meaningful when they are tied to the calendar. *Someday never comes, tomorrow is just a promise.* It's a trite phrase, but somehow, it is simultaneously quite profound.

I learned the calendar lesson a long time ago in my photographic career. I was enduring a long, fallow period in which I had not produced any work for a period of two or three years. I was frustrated and mad at myself. I knew that I needed to get organized, disciplined, and stop the momentum of producing nothing. At the time, I was working a full-time job, teaching photography at night, and had duties as a husband and father to two young children. Obviously, the demands on my time were substantial. I knew I had to be practical about how much photography I could do.

At first, full of enthusiasm, I decided to rededicate myself to photography by spending each weekend in the darkroom. An instant reflection told me this was not practical; it was simply more time than I had to commit. I thought maybe I could print every Saturday. That, too, seemed impractical. I kept cutting back until I decided a reasonable plan was that I could print one Saturday every month and do it religiously without fail.

Then it struck me like a thunderbolt: doing photography one

Saturday every month meant that my photographic life would be limited to twelve days a year – 12/365ths of my life and that was it! That's all the time I had to give to my passion. The absurdity of my priorities was obvious.

If I were a musician, I wouldn't dream of being an accomplished one if I were only willing to pick up my instrument twelve days a year. If I were in business, I couldn't expect profitable success if I worked just one day a month. The only way to be successful in photography is to do it every day! The musician understands as does the businessman, the athlete, the gourmet chef, and the painter.

The question I then had to ask is *what does it mean to be involved in photography every day?* Does this mean I need to be photographing every day? The musician doesn't offer concerts every day. Does it mean I need to be in the darkroom every day? The chef doesn't cook gourmet meals every day. Does it mean I need to be exhibiting every day? The dancer doesn't perform every day. No, being involved in photography every day means simply doing *something* every day. That could be photographing, printing, matting, reading, thinking, looking at photographs, taking notes, talking with other photographers, doing contact sheets – the list could go on indefinitely. Doing photography every day means simply that your life becomes focused by (no pun intended) the lens.

A Completion Strategy

For me, this focus became tangible when I decided to dedicate myself to the completion of four projects every year. I decided that I wanted to complete a project every quarter; that's a lot and I knew I wasn't going to be able to do four *major* projects every year. So, I strategized that I would target for one major project a year and three less intensive ones. Think about it. If a career extends to twenty years, then this strategy creates 20 major projects and 60 secondary projects in a lifetime. That is still a long way from Picasso's 90,000 pieces of finished artwork, but it's not a bad career.

When I began to organize my photographic strategy this way, I found it contained a couple of other unexpected additional benefits. I began to think in terms of *projects* instead of individual photographs. I began to think of projects in their final form, a vision which helped me organize my time into specific tasks. I began to realize the importance of incremental gains on a consistent basis rather than a Herculean effort over the three-day holiday weekend that left me exhausted. I found that certain projects needed a few more images and that helped me organize the time I spent out photographing. I learned that certain projects couldn't be completed until I mastered new technical skills and those realizations helped me broaden my horizons.

A completed project need not be a giant undertaking. It need not be an expensive proposition. It doesn't even require travel expenses or a new lens. All it requires is that you conceive it, execute it and finish it – regardless of its size. A "project" might consist entirely of a well-executed image. It might be a small portfolio of five images. It might be a poster, a web exhibition, a wall exhibition, a CD or DVD, a presentation at your photography group. If you can't finish a large project, finish a small one. If you can't finish an epic poem, write a haiku. In some regards, the smaller the scope of the project, the harder it is to finish because the distillation process is so demanding.

It's amazing what finishing a few projects does to your psyche. When I finished my very first project, it boosted my sense of accomplishment and, therefore, my self-confidence. As my cache of finished projects grew, if I showed someone a body of work and they didn't like it, I could simply show them another project. I now had a number of completed projects to choose from which almost guarantees that I can find something a viewer will like (or buy).

We all know that nature abhors a vacuum. In a tangentially related way, the universe can't stand a completed body of work that doesn't have an audience. If you want to get your work published, exhibited, or sold, the most important thing you can do

– in fact almost the only thing you really *need* to do – is complete a body of work. There are cosmic laws at work here that will not fail you. It's been my experience that simply *doing* creates, as if out of nowhere, the opportunity to get your work *seen*. If you like working in a vacuum, fine. But if you want your work to be seen, it has to be finished, completed, *fini*, q.e.d.

Enough said.

Sixteen

LESSONS FROM JONI MITCHELL

As a child of the late baby boomer generation, the world of music – rock music, in particular – was an important part of my youth. I was too young to attend Woodstock, but I knew the words to all the songs by heart – and still do, even to this day. One of my favorite musicians, now for 24 years, has been Joni Mitchell. As a musician, she's taught me as much about photography as the Ansel Adams photo books ever did.

In 1971, Joni Mitchell released her first album entitled *Songs to a Seagull*. I loved it. I thought it was the best music I'd ever heard. I absorbed the album through repetitive listening so that now every nuance of her music, every guitar riff, every subtlety of her voice is permanently etched so deeply into my brain that I can replay her music in my head today at will. I eagerly awaited her next release with great anticipation. I'd browse the Joni Mitchell album bin in the record store on a weekly basis just so I wouldn't miss its release. Eventually, it arrived.

Her second album was entitled *Blue*. I hated it. It violated my anticipation. It blasphemed my ecstasy over her first album. It, was – and I resented her for this – *different*.

It wasn't just that the *songs* were different songs, but that the entire *mood* of the album was different. Where the first album had been light and full of a folk music sound, the second was all minor chords and dissonant beats. The first was sing-along music. The second was (God forbid) *jazz*. The only redeeming virtues in this second album were one or two songs that I did *kind of* like, on the fringe, but not really.

Nonetheless, I continued to listen to the album from time to time, a bit in anger, a bit in frustration, but subtly intrigued. And then, it started to happen. The more I listened, the more I began to appreciate those dissonant beats and minor chords. The more I listened, the more I began to understand what she was communicating though this music. I listened over and over again and with each revolution of the platter, her new sound screwed its way into my ears. To my surprise, I began to like it, then love it, then consume it with passion. I eventually had to admit that it wasn't so much that the album was *different*, but that the musician had *grown*. Once I realized that her new album wasn't a problem, but was progress, I also realized that my challenge as a listener was to let go of my expectations and to see this second album for what it was. I was challenged to grow with her instead of resisting her progress.

In the last 25 years, Joni Mitchell has created about 20 new albums of music. Each one has been a departure from her previous music. Each one has had a new look, a new feel, a new sound, and is a new creative expression. With every new release I am disappointed, eventually accept the music, and ultimately become wildly enthusiastic about it. In her music she has done what all great artists do – moved, changed, grown.

Notice that I didn't say that her music has *improved*. Improved implies a relative value judgment and such language may be inappropriate or non sequitur when discussing art. I can't say that with every album I think her music has improved. I can say that with every album her creative voice has challenged me to *hear differently*.

Her artistic career has outlined for me an important set of ideas that can be translated to our challenge of being creative with photography. For example:

> She has changed, grown, and built on her
> previous work and successes.

With each new project, I have *not* felt that she was searching for the radical statement needed to feed the demon of a demanding public that demands more outrageous work each times.

She is not being different for the sake of being different – she created difference because these differences are a natural outgrowth of her maturing artistic creativity. As she grows and sees the world differently, so does her music.

With each new project, she is one step ahead of her audience, her listeners. She could have simply found a creative formula that worked (that is, *sold*) and stuck with it by continually giving her audience subtle variations over and over again with each new project. So many artists have done this. She has chosen a different path.

That path places her at an artistic risk with her audience. I suspect that, over the years, she has lost a considerable number of fans due to these constant changes. It's also obvious that with each change she has picked up new fans who have appreciated her new style. That is to say, perhaps her audience is not an identifiable, static group of people, but rather is in constant flux. If not the actual members of her audience, at least her listeners change constantly as they, like I, strive to keep up with her creative variations.

With each new project she has created, Joni Mitchell has defined for herself a distinct project. Her career is not, as is common in other musicians, a series of pop hits. Instead, her career is defined by her exploration of musical themes and styles with each new album. Early in her career she had mostly guitar albums. Later, the piano was her main instrument. She has also explored vocal jazz, synthesizers, conga rhythms and the zither! She has not stood still and this may be her greatest artistic virtue.

It is true that out of these project-oriented works, she has created some popular hits. Well, let me rephrase that. She has not created the pop hits, but rather the media and her fans have created some of her music into pop hits for her. She has simply done her work. I doubt she sees herself as a pop hit songwriter and performer. I suspect that she considers her pop hits more of a fortuitous event than a planned strategy.

There is a certain rebelliousness in all of Joni Mitchell's work. One gets the feeling that she is thumbing her nose a bit at the very pop culture that sustains her. She doesn't create music by pandering to the pop music sales charts. She doesn't create music for the purpose of selling albums, although this is an obvious necessity. Instead, you get the feeling that she creates music based on a personal artistic integrity and would likely do so even if her albums were unsellable.

One of the clues that leads me to this conclusion is that she is a multi-talented artist. In addition to her musical albums, she is also a painter and a photographer. In fact, several of her albums have been decorated with her painting and photographic arts. Although it is possible that she has a parallel career in the visual arts, one gets the feeling that these visual expression are simply another outlet for her artistic spirit.

I find the comparison between her and other artists irresistible. When Milli Vanilli produced their famous lip-sync album, they did so for the purposes of selling music and making money. Only in a perverse way could it be said that they were expressing their "creativity." Joni Mitchell represents the opposite perspective.

It's the difference between the poetry on greeting cards and the poetry of Robert Frost. To call them both "poetry" is an insult to both of them.

One of my favorite photographers is Paul Caponigro. Caponigro first captured my heart with the publication of his book, *Sunflowers*. What a wonderful project this was. What a wonder-

ful creative vision he brought to the project. But, let's be perfectly
honest, not every photograph in this project is a great photograph. In fact, there are a few real clinkers. The same can be said
of Joni Mitchell's musical career – some good albums, some bad
albums, some great albums – and perhaps an occasional song that
is just a plain clinker.

I have followed Caponigro's career, as a fan, just as I have Joni
Mitchell's. With each new book, with each new published work,
Caponigro has continued to challenge my vision. This pattern has
continued right up to his mega-publication, *Megaliths*. I've heard
and read many glowing comments about *Megaliths* and I do not
share this opinion. I've looked at both the book and the special
edition portfolio publication a number of times. Every time I look
at this body of work, I am left with the same impression. It is
exceedingly repetitious, boring, unimaginative, and uninspiring.
In case this last was an obscure statement, I'll clarify it by saying
that I don't like this body of work. However, *and this is the really
important point*, I am absolutely awestruck and in total admiration
of Paul Caponigro's *process*. He is to contemporary photography
what Joni Mitchell is to contemporary music – that is to say,
the consummate explorer, adventurer, changeling. That I might
not appreciate Caponigro's latest work is unimportant to my total
appreciation and applause of Caponigro's artistic career.

With every new published work, Caponigro, like Joni
Mitchell, takes a certain risk with his relationship to his audience's
demands. All artists repeat this same process. This implies
a strategic question that every artist should strive to answer.
*Should this risk be managed and contained OR accepted as a part of
the job description?*

Artists like Cher (in the musical world) and Ansel Adams
(in the photographic world) share a different creative path. Cher
and Adams had, early in their career, an extraordinary creative
vision, unlike any other creative vision in their respective fields.
That, in itself, deserves our admiration and support. But unlike
Caponigro and Mitchell, once their vision was codified, they
spent the rest of their careers creating work after work that was

derivative of their original creative vision. Please don't misinterpret this. It is not that I intend to disparage Cher and Adams for their lack of creative growth. We should all be so lucky as to have the kinds of creative visions they had, even if only once in our life. The lesson to be learned here is simply that there are a variety of creative paths. The path of change and risk, the path of creative and artistic growth, the path of exploration and experimentation is a choice that can be made once in a career (as in Cher or Adams) or repeatedly as a life-long commitment to artistic vision (as in Caponigro or Mitchell). For me, the quintessential artist is the individual whose artistic path is defined not by their product, but rather by their life. Whereas Adams and Cher found a product that determined their life, Caponigro and Mitchell have a life that determines their product.

There is an extremely delicate balance between creativity and expectation. As Cher's career evolves (and as Adams' did) with each new product, book, or musical album, it has been difficult to maintain a sense of anxious anticipation. Their works are far too repetitious to expect anything particularly new or exciting. Bigger, yes. A more extreme version of their previous work, yes. Each in their own way continue to push the envelope with every product. They just push the envelope of the same theme farther and farther.

Artists like Caponigro and Mitchell are different than this. They push a different envelope. They don't push the envelope of the *theme* as much as they push the envelope of *their own creative vision*.

In truth, the ideas in this article have as much to do with the responsibility of an audience as they do with the creative process of an artist. A case could be made that an audience has no responsibility to an artist whatsoever – that responsibility is exclusively a one-way street from the artist *to* the audience. This unfortunate and all too common perspective is quite destructive to art, and to artists. The modern audience's appetite for bigger, more extravagant and simply more of the same is a seductive siren. The struggling artist, often struggling for years and decades, finally lands upon a formula that gains a certain critical and particularly economic success. By harboring expectations of consistency, the audience lures the creative artist to abandon the path of exploration and instead reproduce the formula that has finally secured bread for their table and gratification for their soul. To paraphrase DeTocqueville, "A peoples get the art they deserve." It requires an unbelievable act of faith and will to resist this temptation and instead continue the path of creative exploration. Joni Mitchell could easily have made a career spanning decades creating nothing but variations of her popular hit song, *Chelsea Morning*. Paul Caponigro could have become the world's most famous photographer of ever-so-many varieties of plants.

We should learn from them, admire them, honor them and thank them for choosing an alternative, much more creative path. In doing so we have a responsibility to allow them the occasional less-than-successful work. My responsibility to Caponigro is to remain faithful in spite of the fact that I find his *Megaliths* work uninspired and disappointing. I wait with eager anticipation for his next creative vision and I can allow him to find his way through his creative process. To do otherwise is to consign myself to the role of the fickle audience – a fate that simply punishes me for my impatience – and consigns Caponigro to the path of the "has been" or the formula repeater.

The reason I admire and appreciate Joni Mitchell so much, you see, is that she has not only shown me the path of the creative artist, but she has also taught me, through the lessons of *audience*, a great deal about me. What more could I ask from a creative artist? How better could she have influenced my life?

Seventeen

TWENTY YEARS TO BREAK THE RULES

Lessons from the Made of Steel *Folios*

A creative endeavor is almost never a straight path, never predictable, and often clearly seen only in retrospect. In this essay I'm going to allow myself a bit of personal retrospection. I will describe a creative path that eventually led me, through several lessons, to the *Made of Steel* Folios. I don't like to be so self-indulgent, but I am hoping that examining my process in this specific example might be a useful exercise in understanding the dynamic process of creativity – as it was lived – since this project unfolded in such unexpected ways.

In the 1970s and early 80s, I was photographing landscapes, almost exclusively. On an impulse, while out photographing one day in 1982, I wandered into an old machine shop in Port Townsend, Washington – Dollar's Garage. I asked permission to make a photograph and the proprietor, Mr. Dollar, agreed. I spent the next six hours photographing his tool bench, his shop, and the artifacts of his trade. (Unfortunately, I didn't ask to make his portrait.) Little did I know that this impulsive whim would lead to one of the major photographic projects of my life. **Lesson #1:** It's amazing how many times big things sneak up on us and take us completely by surprise.

After I developed the negatives and contact sheets from Dollar's Garage, I looked at them more carefully. I realized how many *potential* images I'd ignored – small compositions that I could now see buried in the details of the larger views on my contact sheets. I became fascinated with small machine shops, garages, and the men who work with metal and steel. For the next 19 years, as I traveled around the country, I found such businesses – such men – everywhere I went. I started photographing them with regularity, focusing on details and compositions that I responded to intuitively. I had no idea, at the time, that I was creating a photographic project. I was just following my intuition, photographing at will, allowing myself to be fascinated with the subject material, wherever it led me. **Lesson #2:** Playing without purpose is sometimes a highly creative virtue.

During the 1980s, I was deeply involved in a photographic group that met monthly to share images and learn from each other. I started showing this work at those meetings and was surprised at the two reactions I received: *Why was I printing this work in a warm, brown tone?* (I was even asked if I was trying to make fake "old-looking" images!); and *Why was I photographing these stupid tools?* Nobody, with very few exceptions, appreciated the early work (and they may have been right). At the time, in my naiveté, I found this lack of encouragement fueled my self-doubt. **Lesson #3:** Critics are everywhere and constructive suggestions quite rare. It's too bad, but it is often true that other photographers can be the least encouraging. In retrospect, I see I had found **Lesson #4:** Discouragement, setbacks, and self-doubt are a reality that accompany *every* creative endeavor. Each time I photographed in a machine shop, I wondered if I should be out in the landscape. Luckily, my impulse to photograph in machine shops was stronger than my self-doubt, so I kept photographing tools and grease and having a ball. **Lesson #5:** It is handy if you can be your own cheerleader.

The breakthrough came in an unexpected way. I was invited to show a body of work to a group of people who were *not* photographers. After some vacillation, I decided to show these photographs of the old shops and tools. Not one of these people asked why I had brown-toned the images, what lens I used, what film or developer, or which reciprocity table I employed. Not one questioned why I was photographing these things. Instead, they asked me about the people in the photographs and my experiences of photographing them. **Lesson #6:** Show your work to people outside your group of photographic friends – the response will be interesting.

I was surprised at how easily I was able to recall stories, incidents, moments, sometimes just a phrase that had impressed me while I was photographing. For the first time, as I showed the photographs I told stories of these men and their work – and to my amazement and delight, people laughed and smiled, people *reacted* and looked more closely at the images. Their relationship to my images had been deepened by the stories I told. It was a revelation to me. It was more than a revelation, it was a *revolution.* **Lesson #7:** I suddenly realized that my potential as a storyteller – as a photographer – was not diminished by words, but could be *enhanced* by them. For this body of work – not for *every* body of work, but for this one – I recognized the importance of the text.

Later, I received an invitation to exhibit some work at a local nonprofit gallery. Emboldened by my previous storytelling experience, I decided to risk an experiment. I condensed and distilled the stories into a few sentences, a quote, or a quick observation – a sentence or two of text for each image. I then printed the text on pieces of paper which were then matted along with the photograph in a single frame, the photograph and the text each in their individual window. Certainly this was not a new idea in photography, but it was new to me – a photographer whose heroes had been the great West Coast photographers that had espoused the pure print, the white mat board, and the ubiquitous title "Untitled." Most photographers in this vein eschewed text as being not just unnecessary, but an *insult* to the photograph. I had been taught the maxim that *any photograph that needs text is a bad photograph because it can't stand on its own.* My personal revelation was to realize that (**Lesson #8**) such inflexible – albeit unwritten – rules are always counterproductive to the creative life. By breaking this rule about text,

I found these photographs connected with an audience in ways that were not possible without it.

I exhibited 38 images with their text components and attended the opening, like all artists do, slightly holding my breath with butterflies dancing the Lindy in the pit of my stomach. It was the noisiest opening in an art gallery I have ever attended! It was noisy because people were *talking* about the photographs, *reminiscing* about their great Uncle Bob who used to have a machine shop, *laughing* out loud at the stories they read, pausing for *minutes at a time* before each image, finishing the exhibition and starting all over again with the first photograph to go through it a second time. Never before, and rarely since, have I seen such reactions from an audience in an art gallery. To my surprise, I found I was thrilled that people were ignoring the artifact and engaging the artwork. **Lessons #9 and #10:** Never overlook the importance of content; it's what the audience relates to, not your artistic struggle or process. I also learned the difference between artists and normal people – whom a friend of mine calls *civilians*. Artists care about the artwork in the artifacts. The rest of the folks care about the *life* in the artwork.

Many people at the opening asked if I had a book they could buy – they wanted to share what they had seen, maybe offer their friends or a family member a gift. **Lesson #11:** When people connect with art, they want to own it or give it as a gift. I had always thought people buy artwork to support a struggling artist. **Lesson #12:** When "civilians" purchase art, it is because of their connection with the *artwork*, not their connection with the *artist*. Unfortunately, I didn't have a book nor the capital to publish one. Because I couldn't afford to publish a book I began to explore alternatives, and, as the maxim goes, necessity is the mother of invention.

I realized immediately that this project had three inherent limitations. First, this was not wall art – not pretty picture landscapes, not large prints – so the traditional image-in-white-mat-board and frame seemed silly. Second, individual images, stripped of the context of their brothers and sisters, were weakened by being isolated from the group. Third, the text was essential to the project and to the individual images! I knew this body of work needed to be exhibited and packaged as such. A book would have been ideal, but I had to think smaller. I had to think about producing something in my darkroom, in smaller quantities that I could produce on my own and within my budget. Essentially, I found myself asking: Could I make a book in the darkroom?

Here is where the creative crisis really occurred. I was taught that photographs don't need text, but this work from the machine shops seemed to sing when the text was included. I was taught the photograph is better when it's bigger, but this work was not wall art nor décor, and seemed to shine when it was small, intimate, handheld. I was taught that a photograph was supposed to be presented overmatted in a pristine white mat board, dry-mounted, signed in the lower right hand corner and overmatted with a four-ply beveled mat. But this work seemed to drown in such overproduction. I was taught that great photographs were selenium toned, but these images worked best in warm-tones. Now, I'm not rebellious by nature; by nature I respect my elders and betters. Who was I to question the wisdom of those great photographers from the Monterey Peninsula, or Alfred Stieglitz, or *all* of my contemporaries who followed the wisdom that had become codified as *fine art photography* in 20th Century? But here it was – **Lesson #13** – that in order for this work to mature into something I was proud of, something that connected with real people, it seemed I needed to break almost every rule of photography that I had ever learned. I just needed to give myself permission to do so.

I should say that I was *not* deluded into thinking that *because* I was breaking the rules the work was good. This is an all-too-common mistake of beginners. Rather I should say that in spite of breaking the rules this was the way the work needed to be done. I always caution new photographers that the first task is to learn the rules thoroughly; master the tried and true. Only then will breaking the rules make sense. **Lesson #14:** The trick is to know the rules, but not be frozen by them; use the rules wisely, but know that breaking them is also a form of using them. What has amazed me since then is how many times I've seen other photographers' work that would benefit by breaking out of the codified, gallery-approved rules of presentation. Too often I see the seed of brilliant photographic work stuffed into a codified form that kills it. Nice tones and a clean mat, but vacant and hollow. I want to kindly approach these photographers and shout WAKE UP!

I'm not an extremist about this, honestly. There's nothing wrong with white mat board and an image plopped in the middle, slightly above center, with the artist's signature in the lower right hand corner. I like such work – I even still make such work. But it's not the *only* way to make photographs or artwork that is based in photography. **Lesson #15:** It's not heretical to be creative. What's the worst that can happen? Stupid artwork! But maybe, just maybe, some people might connect with your creative vision and see what you are trying to create/reflect/say/ transmit with your photography. And if you only end up making stupid artwork, well, as they say: even the person who falls flat on their face is at least moving forward.

I screwed up my courage and started to let my imagination run. What if I put the text *in* the photograph? How would one do that? Thankfully I learned **Lesson #16:** Look outside photographic circles for solutions that can be joined with traditional photography. I learned I could have a service bureau output text on graphic arts film which could be subsequently contact printed in the darkroom on photographic paper. I learned about "stripping" – the process of finely positioning graphic arts film with the use of pin registration. Using these new tools, it was possible to enlarge my original negatives in the darkroom as I had always done, and then expose my text components in the photographic emulsion itself! When the paper was processed in the chemistry, the image and the text would both be developed in the emulsion.

I was encouraged and got even bolder. What if I then added a short story printed on a few pages of art paper? What if the images were printed with generous borders in the photographic paper that didn't need mat board? I'd need some sort of a cover to hold all of this. How would I do that?

All of these questions opened the door to the creation of small "portfolios" of photographs with text. These small, book-like productions allowed me to create an intimate product without the necessity of a full-blown book project. In 1991, I created a short-run edition of three such folios, all titled *Made of Steel*. The first folio was *The Portraits*, the second *The Shops*, and the third *The Tools*. Each folio had its own cover and a selection of five images from the full exhibition.

The project took *months* to complete. Each image was exposed with appropriate dodging, burning, and flashing and then a second exposure for the text and a third exposure for the key-line around the photographs. Each image required incredible precision and hours and hours to complete the edition run. They were tortuous to make and expensive to produce. I'm not averse to hard work, but there are limits beyond which only the stupid will go. I decided to use *creative thought* rather than *brute perseverance* to see if I could find a better way.

Lesson #17: There is, indeed, more than one way to skin a cat. I began to wonder if the film used in graphic arts for *text* could be adapted for use in a traditional photographic darkroom for the production of *images* as well. What if I could create a perfect photographic negative that could be printed simultaneously with the text? If I could figure it out, I could create these folios so much more easily! Three years of experimenting and I had a working method to be able to do it. This was actually the tiny seed that started me on the technological path that lead, eventually, to the LensWork *Special Editions Collection*.

Now, two decades after that first photograph in Dollar's Garage, I finally get to come full circle. After 21 years of exploring and experimenting, fumbling and stumbling around, the technology and my skills have caught up with my creative vision. I can now produce the *Made of Steel* folios as I had hoped to do – an edition of exquisite little folios without killing myself in the process.

I never would have guessed that the photograph I made in Dollar's Garage in 1982 would lead me down such a convoluted and unexpected path. How could I know that it would challenge my notions of creativity, of photographic aesthetics, of a photograph's accessibility to an audience? But this creative challenge has been one my most exciting adventures as a photographer. In fact (**Lesson #18**), I've concluded that *creativity* and *challenge* are intimately integrated. It is not possible to have one without the other. A life of art *is* a life of challenge – of overcoming – of doing what cannot be done. If it can be done easily, if it requires no challenge, it probably is not art.

So now I produce these little "folios" as one of my fundamental art forms. I still make the occasional piece of wall art, but they are rare. I say *one of my fundamental art forms* because breaking-out of the plop-in-the-white-mat-board tradition was more mind-expanding than I originally thought. I didn't just replace mat board with folio covers – I replaced a single form with *anything I could dream up!* Image and text, image and graphics, image with a physical object montage, images that hang by strings, images in Japanese *tanzaku* or *shikishi* frames, images on CDs, websites, images with audio – the possibilities are limitless. **Lesson #19:** Be careful of allowing yourself the freedom of creativity; it might just shatter the limits of everything you now know. Creativity – the life of an artist – is not for the timid. You might find that you make some pretty awful art – on this trust me, I know. And not everyone will like or respect (or buy, or understand) your work. *It's not in a white mat board!* But you will find that (**Lesson #20**) there are those who will "get it" and it is for these people and for yourself that you create. It is for the process of exploring and finding, failing and finding, finding and sharing that you create.

My idea about folios may not be a useful idea for anyone else and I'm not recommending or suggesting that folios are a replacement to the traditional presentation of photographs. The traditional presentation is, still, the *traditional* one. But, I am suggesting that the creative path sometimes leads in different directions – if we are open to it. I am also suggesting that it may be possible for photography – for fine art photography – to be a great deal more than a rectangular print in white mat board.

It seems that learning and letting go are the twin rails of the creative path. They are fueled by patience and perseverance – these four characteristics are in a continual interplay. They are an important foundation of the creative process. Funny how such an instantaneous art form as photography can take more than 20 years to materialize a final product. I find this more understandable when I realize that it is *me* that must learn and let go, and *me* that must be patient and persevere. To be an artist is to *become* an artist, and this is a process that unfolds in its own time, continually yet inconsistently, but more readily if we recognize our role and open ourselves to the work.

As Tolkien cautions us in *The Hobbit*, paths are wondrous things because we never know where they might lead us. That is the very the reason to take them.

Eighteen

RANDOM THOUGHTS

Over the years, I've gathered quite a few snippets of thought about photography. I usually scribble these moments of insight on little scraps of paper and stuff them in a folder labeled *Random Thoughts On Photography*. When I need to jump-start my creativity or shake out of a rut, I scan through the folder. The following is an eclectic sample of ideas that I've decided to publish here for no other reason than it helps me justify keeping these scraps of paper so long.

Here goes …

•

I have two cats, both of them the same breed. They are Korats from Thailand – a small, all-gray breed. When friends come over they can never tell them apart and I'm consistently amazed at this. In fact, my friends wonder how I tell them apart! But to me the two cats, although similar, are as different as can be. I'm sure this comes from living with them on a daily basis. I see the subtleties that separate them; my friends see the similarities that make them the same.

This must be true for photography, too. Working with a given subject matter again and again teaches the eye to see the subtleties that aren't apparent at first sight. This ability to distinguish is not an act of will; it is a *result of experience*, careful examination, and a certain degree of concentration and involvement with the subject over time.

One frightening implication is that this might also be true for those who look at our photographs. As photographers, we see differently; the subtleties of tones and details that make a photograph sing for us might be completely invisible to our audience. We might marvel at qualities that are simply invisible to others. I once had a gallery owner tell me that almost no one who visited his gallery could see the difference between a silver print and a platinum print until he pointed out the tonal and density differences to them!

•

As artists, we are supposed to be willing to sacrifice a great deal for our art. Yet, the demands of a *sacrifice* are never-ending. How much should I be willing to sacrifice for my art? I'm not willing to die for a photograph. I am willing to be uncomfortable making one. Somewhere in between the two is the line that defines the limit I am willing to endure to make art. I should choose my limits with care and purpose. If I am not pragmatic about both the sacrifices and the limits, it will be too easy to feel guilty or become lazy.

For example, in the darkroom I know it is essentially impossible to make a *perfect* print. Every print can be improved. At what point do I stop? This is a critical question that every photographer must decide.

•

It's funny how the artist's signature influences a print. It shouldn't, but it does. If I look at a photograph and see that it was done by a "Master Photographer" I'm often predisposed to assume that it's a better photograph than it really is. Conversely, if the signature indicates the artist is no one I've heard of, my work for its merit, it's important to be aware of this bias and, when possible, not to let it interfere.

•

Intellectually, I know there is absolutely no relationship

between how easy or hard it is to make a photograph and how good it is. Nonetheless, every photographer's natural tendency is to diminish the prints that came easily and overvalue the ones that required Herculean efforts.

•

Every time I attend a lecture on photography, I've been glad I went – I learn a new idea or two, regardless of the speaker's identity. Every time I attend a lecture on painting, on sculpture, on music, on poetry, on writing, on woodworking, or on dance I am challenged, stimulated, boggled, slapped upside my head and habits, spun around and walk away thinking I need to begin my art education from the beginning. I wish I had paid better attention in art class and read as many books about the other arts as I have about photography. I could have avoided so many pitfalls and mistakes that the other artists learned long ago.

•

I've noticed that my method of photographing in the landscape has changed considerably over the last 20 years. I used to drive through the landscape at 50mph, searching for a good subject from the corners of my eyes. As a technique it worked, but lately it seems that this method has become less functional for me. Now, I have more success when I stop the car, walk around, soak-up a place, study it leisurely, and then make a series of photographs, often within a hundred yards of the car. In fact, this technique seems to work so well it almost makes no difference *where* I stop the car. I wonder if this is an observation about youth in general, or only about me?

•

When I began photography, my photographs were all gray and pasty. For the longest time, I thought the magic was in getting a great Dmax black. In the next phase, my prints were way too contrasty and dark – black and white with hardly any grays to speak of. Now that I'm older and a much better printer,

I find that all the magic in a photograph is in the grays. I've come back to where I started but it is certainly not the same place.

•

made horrible photographs. Over the course of ten years, I bought all kinds of new equipment and saw very little improvement in my photographs. When I finally learned how to see, I got rid of most of my equipment and my images improved dramatically.

Said a parallel way, when I started photography, I didn't really feel like a photographer because all of my equipment fit into a small camera bag. I started to feel like a serious photographer when I carried several cases of equipment, a rolling cart and a big photographer's vest into the landscape. I started making good photographs when I got rid of most it. While it may seem puzzling, the answer may be as simple as this: after I got rid of so much equipment, I spent my time managing my vision rather than managing my stuff.

•

It's too bad the apprentice system has died-out in photography. There is no doubt in my mind that the best way to learn photography is to become an assistant to someone who really knows what they are doing. Then just watch them, study them, absorb from them, and keep your big mouth shut for a long, long time.

•

The process of being a photographer is to work diligently to minimize the degradation in each step from conception to the final result. The subject is always better than the vision in my mind's eye; the vision in my mind's eye is always better than the negative; the negative is always better than the print; and the print is almost always a disappointment. Each step along the way introduces a little more degradation. The trick is to manage and minimize this slippage from vision to print. The devil is in the details.

•

The process of being an artist is to forget everything that you know and to really see, with eyes that are simultaneously naïve and sophisticated.

•

As a general rule of thumb, photographers who insist they cannot say anything of importance about their photographs should try more diligently to do so. Those who insist on talking about their photographs should refrain from doing so at all costs.

•

One of the deadliest traps in photography is defined by current trends. In certain group-think herds, this mentality might be useful – for example, in team sports or the military. But, when an artist follows the herd, he just ends up looking foolish with cookie-cutter results. As a case in point, when it comes to photographing jumping dancers in mid-air, Lois Greenfield did it brilliantly, but everyone else's just look, well, wrong.

•

For years I've noticed that I see some of my best photographs when I'm really tired. I believe this has something to do with the natural quieting of my thoughts and the cessation of my tendency to intellectualize about my images. Thinking non-thinking is the key. When I quiet my mind, it's as though I hear and see better. When I insist on thinking, my pictures always look contrived.

•

There is a great benefit to being organized and almost no benefit to being disorganized. I never leave the darkroom messy or the trays unwashed. I label and file my negatives immediately after they are dry. I organize my computer files religiously. I keep printing notes on every print. I number, categorize, sequence, order, file, clean, pick-up and systematize everything. I may be fastidious about this, but I find it allows me to focus my thoughts on the creative process rather than searching for something I can't find and desperately need. Worse, every time I get sloppy, I re-learn the value of this lesson all over again.

•

If the history of photography teaches us anything, it is that the tools we use to make photographs are constantly changing and becoming obsolete. (Who now uses wet plates?) So, why all the fuss about new equipment? And, why all the fuss about digital?

As Sister Wendy says, the progress of art – unlike technology – is not built up like an ever higher-reaching ladder. A calculator is better than an abacus which is better than counting on your fingers – there is a linear progression of technology that improves with each new advance. This is not true in art. Albumen prints are not better than silver prints which are not better than ink-jet prints, nor the other way around. They are all just different. A given image might look better as a silver print or as a platinum print, but platinum *as a medium* is not inherently better than silver *as a medium*, nor are these better *as a medium* than the newer technologies. In all cases, the sensitivity of the artist is the key – not the medium.

•

Why is it that when a group of photographers get together they always talk about cameras and lenses – or now, cameras and software? I can count on one hand the number of times I've had conversations over dinner or drinks with other photographers where the conversation is about images. The exception to this is in a workshop setting. Maybe this is why I like going to workshops so much. In fact, the minute I hear someone ask

"What lens did you use?" or ask about the film, I intuitively know I am talking to a copycat or a novice.

•

We each have five senses – sight, hearing, smell, taste, and touch. The best photographers seem to be the ones who don't ignore the other four. Think of Brett Weston, Minor White, and Eugene Smith just to name a few. Their reputation as sensualists is almost as great as their reputation as photographers. I can't help but wonder if there is some connection at some deep level.

•

If I had to restrict myself to just one activity that would improve my photography the most, what would that be? Without a doubt, I should *finish* more of my work.

•

I agree with Oliver Gagliani that photography took a giant step backwards when money got involved. Not that there is anything wrong with money, but some photographers see the twin seducers – money and fame – as not only as their *right*, rather than as a *reward* for a lifetime of achievement. That you choose to make art does not mean that you accomplished anything. I might choose to make dinner, but this does not make me a chef. I might choose to play an instrument, but I am certainly not good at it. No one has a right to have their work exhibited, published, purchased, or admired. These results are all earned and rewarded, not guaranteed.

•

I've concluded that I cannot make good photographs with my friends in tow. When I go out photographing with my friends, I am too interested and diverted by conversation and camaraderie to make meaningful images. I wish this weren't so, but in looking back on my 30 years in photography, I find it true. My best images seem to be those that I made after being out photograph-ing all alone for more than a few days. It takes a while to drop-off the concerns of daily life and get into a creative and receptive frame of mind. Professionals cannot afford this luxury and per-haps there is something I can learn from them.

•

Photography can be such a fun hobby. But, I find artmak-ing is completely different from a hobby. A hobby is a diversion, a vacation, a relaxation, pastime – i.e., a way to pass the time. Artmaking is a battle, a confrontation, a pursuit, a matter of the soul and survival, a passion, a pile of frustration and a grain of reward, an irresistible impulse, an addiction, a form of self-imposed insanity in a world that does not require me to make art at all. My art is, therefore, a great joy simply because it is of no use whatsoever to anyone at any time. In fact, if it had a great purpose, I would find it work.

A hobby is a collective activity. Artmaking is solitary. A hobby is about stuff. Artmaking is about the soul. A hobby gives us a break from everyday life. Artmaking is the core of everyday life. Grocery shopping is real and the hobby is time-off from reality. Artmaking is real and groceries are time-off. Photography can be both. I find I slip back and forth and my relationship with my camera changes from season to season, from year to year. Sometimes it is a hobby. Sometimes it is my mentor. Sometimes it is my master. I used to feel guilty being a hobbyist and tortured being an artmaker. Now I see it as a spectrum – and I can move around in the spectrum as I choose. Photography is just a tool – as hammers can hang pictures or build houses. It is not the tool that defines the challenge; the individual and his decisions define the challenge and the nature of the project.

•

Glass is the most marvelous and amazing thing! It can be clear or smoky, distorted or transparent, bend light as a lens or reflect light as a mirror. It can be cleaned to a spotless, invisible nothing. It can be ground to a diffusing glow. It can be colored and thereby color the entire world. It can be shaped, bent, folded, stretched, hollow or solid, thin or thick. It is the first and most important part of the photographer's tool that actually touches the light. If glass can be all these things, how much more so *the photographer's mind.*

Nineteen

TOOLS

I am thinking about purchasing a new camera and am traumatized by the process.

Worse yet, I was surprised that thinking about a new camera system was such a traumatic combination of thoughts. I was so fascinated by my own fears of buying a new camera system – once I realized why I felt anxious – that I couldn't help but wonder what lie at the root of these fears. Exploring these fears started me thinking about *tools*.

In the normal way of thinking, the tool is simply a device that the mind uses to amplify itself. We use a microphone and an amplifier to increase the volume of our voice, and the tool gives us the power to communicate beyond the limitations of the human body. The automobile is a tool that allows us to travel across vast distances, again overcoming the limitations of the human body. The screwdriver is a tool that concentrates the power in our hands to the point of impact with a screw. Normally speaking, this use of tools dominates the way we think about them; they are simply a means of taking our own thoughts and activities and amplifying them, perhaps using them more efficiently or powerfully. The objective is defined by previous thoughts and the tool helps turn these thoughts into reality. This kind of use for the tool – for the camera – does not, essentially, make me uncomfortable. But there is another way in which tools affect our lives.

Tools are not only a means to amplify our own minds. They are, in fact, devices that *change and affect our thought processes*.

Once the use of a software program was reasonably understood, the knowledge of how to use it opened up unforeseen possibilities for the creation of new products and new results that could not possibly have been imagined prior to knowing the software. In essence, the software changed the way I think! This is the subtle use of tools.

This idea has been well-documented and discussed at length in relationship to photography. Think how the introduction of a hand-held camera changed the way photographers looked at the world. Think of how the introduction of roll film changed the way photographers could relate to the world, and in particular the way photographers were able to travel and photograph more exotic locations. Tools change the way we think, change the way we perceive, change the way we produce, and change the way and direction of our progress. This is what traumatizes me about purchasing a new camera system.

The camera I'd used for the vast majority of my photography was an old, pre-World War II Arca Swiss monorail medium-format camera that shoots 6x9 cm images on 120 film. For a view camera, it's quite portable, but does have all the limitations that view cameras normally have: it's bulky, it requires a tripod, it's a slow process to make any image, and requires considerable precision and attention to focusing the lens. Despite these limitations, I have become comfortable with these procedures and this camera has dominated my work for twenty years.

The reason I began thinking of abandoning this as my primary camera was that it is best used as a "safari-camera," and by that I mean that I am out in the world, with the camera, dedicated to doing photography and *only* photography. When I go out to photograph, I pack up the camera, several boxes of accessories, film, a dark cloth, the view camera lenses, my camera vest, and fill my trunk with gear. Then I head out into the landscape, or small-town America, or some other locale of interest and begin the process of looking for a photograph. Because I am "on safari" this kind of work is best done when I have several days to dedicate to photographing. The long weekend, the week's vacation, the extended trip have been a primary source for photographing. When I was younger, I had the time to regularly go out into the world and photograph this way. Now that I am older and involved in other activities – particularly in my role as editor and publisher of *LensWork* – I find I have significantly less time for this kind of safari activity. Instead, my ability to find time for photography now faces a challenge. It seems that whenever I have the camera – on those rare occasions when I do get out – the conditions, subject matter, light, or my mind may not be conducive to making the kinds of images I would like. On the other hand, when the light is right, the inspiration whetted, and the moment in front of me, I never seem to have a camera! The tool I have used for all these years is no longer functional for my vision. I now need a camera that goes with me everywhere, every day, and is with me when I see a photograph and have only minutes or hours to photograph.

So, I am searching for a new tool but, here is the rub: I know that the kinds of tools I'm considering are going to change my imagery, change the way I see the world, change my well-defined and comfortable photographic perspective – *and this terrifies me.* What will I see with a hand-held camera? How will my perception of the world change with an auto-focus tool? My God, comfort zones are powerful prisons!

Once I began to think about this innate fear, I realized how absolutely necessary it was for me to make this leap. The very fact that my eye has been so trained by my camera is almost an indictment of my single-camera strategy over the last twenty years. There is something about simply having a new tool that gives the mind permission to think in ways that it previously didn't. The mind would not otherwise allow itself to do so. This unwillingness of the mind to engage change eventually results in a frustration and a limitation or lack of vision.

Tools also have a unique characteristic of being used by different people in different ways. The tool is not only a means for a person to create, but also a means by which the character of the tool-user is revealed. The craftsman uses the tool and the tool shapes and fashions the craftsman. Some people can take a tool and turn its use into something wonderful, while others use the same tool and produce something that isn't. This, also, is a key to my resistance to a new tool. I know, intuitively, that the photographic success I've had with my old tools may not translate smoothly (or at all) into a new tool. I've developed a certain reputation for being a photographer of some accomplishment – at least in the minds of some – but if I pick up a new tool and it reveals a different character in me, I might expose a side of myself that is a failure photographically. I might stumble and damage my precious reputation. At least, that's what the self-conscious mind thinks.

The truth is, of course, that this fear is the great enemy of the creative life. Intellectually at least, I know that my engaging a new tool may present challenges but it is absolutely necessary and, in fact is the very definition the creative life. Without the challenge of learning a new tool, and thereby learning a bit more about ourselves, we stifle the creative life. The camera is simply an extension of my mind. It is a vehicle to communicate. Each camera, each set of tools, contains its own inherent grammar and vocabulary. I know that when I abandon my monorail and pick up a hand-held camera, I will need to learn a new vocabulary, a new way of seeing, a new way of communicating and my deepest fear is that I might find I have nothing to communicate. Of course, the self-defeating logic contained in this idea is simply that if I don't pick up the new camera and I don't begin seeing the world in a new way that I will not communicate at all. Not communicating is functionally the same as not having anything to communicate. As Mark Twain said, "Those who don't read have no advantage over those who can't."

In a slightly different way, I've practiced this challenge for years. I regularly browse through stores that have nothing to do with my interests or regular routines. I wander through a fabric store just to see if there are ideas or products there that might be solutions for something in my life that has nothing to do with sewing. For example, I found a fantastic print-flattening weight in the form of a cast iron barbecue griddle. It's a big, hefty, flat piece of rolled steel with turned-up edges. Perfect for the darkroom; but found in the barbecue store!

I know this technique of looking for the unexpected solution in the unexpected location – I know it because I use it in other areas. I guess it's just about time that I applied this knowledge to the purchase of a new camera.

Twenty

LETTING GO
OF THE CAMERA

You've probably heard the apocryphal story about Edward Weston in which he supposedly received a series of proofs for a book addressed to "Edward Weston, Artist." The story goes that he returned the proofs in the same envelope after scratching out the word *Artist* and writing above it the word *Photographer.* We are supposed to conclude that he was making a statement that to be a photographer was a different thing (and perhaps better thing) than being an artist. If this is, indeed, what he meant, I believe he missed the point.

Photography's bitter relationship with art, and the resulting feud between photographers and other artists, is a long and boring story the roots of which lie in the ridiculous assumption that photography is realistic and painting, for example, is personal expression. This common assumption makes – well, you know what it makes – out of *u* and *me.*

The argument that photography is a realistic art is a specious one because (with this even Edward Weston would have to agree) the world is not monochromatic, not two dimensional, not limited to the color palette of photographic media, not still, and not that small. Why a 16x20 inch, black and white landscape is considered more realistic than a three-foot by four-foot, color landscape painting is merely a conventional perspective and not related to any truth. The idea that photography is truthful is certainly false. You need only search for Ansel Adams' Yosemite. Trust me, I've been there, and it exists only in his pictures.

The absence of absolute truth in photography is particularly difficult to remember when one is looking at (supposedly) documentary photography. Consider the classic image by Dorothea Lange, *Migrant Mother*. How easy it is to interpret a sense of hopelessness and a future of despair from the photograph. Thankfully, Florence Thompson (the subject of the famous photograph) enjoyed a brighter future than the photographs suggests will be possible for her. Her story is told in the book *Dust Bowl Descent* by Bill Ganzel, who photographed her and her daughters in 1976. She lived to an advanced age, solidly affixed in middle class comfort. Photographic truth is usually a constructed, believable fiction or, as in Lange's photograph, a complex symbol that doesn't represent absolute truth either.

Let me state this again so it doesn't get lost: Photographic truth, more often than not, is a constructed, believable fiction. It is believable that the sky was that dark and dramatic but it may actually have been darkened by such simple darkroom techniques as burning-in or filtration on the camera lens. When we look at an Ansel Adams landscape of Yosemite Valley, we believe the air is that clear when it *isn't*, even though it perhaps *was* – at the moment when Ansel Adams clicked the shutter.

If it's so easy to demonstrate conclusively that photography is a fiction, then why are we photographers clinging to this myth and notion about truthfulness? I would propose that, quite simply, we are clinging to *absolution from the responsibility of self-expression*. Said another way, we don't want to be expressive, like the painters, because we might have nothing to say or only trivialities to reveal. We hide behind objectivity. When our photographs are objective, the meaningless photograph is then the result of a faulty subject, not our own inadequacies.

This is precisely why photographing is so often the search for subject material. Proof: The last time you "went out photographing," what did you spend your time doing? Did you drive around looking for something to photograph? Is it possible you were looking for a *thing* that was worth photographing – as opposed to an emotion that was worth expressing?

When a landscape photographer shows us a photograph, they are inherently saying "this thing is significant." When a painter shows us a painting, they are inherently saying "this emotion is significant." When Andrew Wyeth painted Helga he was not trying to prove that Helga was important, but that Helga was important *to him.* The first is a supposedly objective statement of reality; the second is a totally subjective statement of personal value. By using his craft effectively, he hoped to make Helga important to *us,* and that is the purpose of his artwork.

Here is my proposal to you. You may choose, as a photographer, to play the self-delusional objectivity game – lots of photographers do it. Realize, however, that your photographs are no less subjective, no less fiction, no less of a construction than Cubist, Impressionist and Surrealist paintings. Edward Weston was wrong; a photographer *is* an artist, and the photographs you make are personal fictions much more than they are objective facts.

Photographic truth and objectivity are myths. All photographs are constructed, edited, distilled, morphed, abstracts of reality that are the product of manipulations to show what the artist wants viewers to see.

It is understandable that this is a difficult and uncomfortable truth for most photographers. It is easy to *record;* technology makes it easier every decade. It is much more difficult to feel, to interpret, to express – and technology doesn't help with that at all. Tuning the piano is entirely different from composing or playing the music.

There are those who fear we are now on the verge of a technological tide that will sweep away the last vestiges of this "truth and objectivity" myth. We are. But my candid observation of this fear is that it has little to do with technology and a great deal to do with the challenge of being an artist today. Artmaking is not about gadget manipulation or image manipulation. Artmaking is a thing of the soul. This is the biggest reason so many photographers get caught up in the technological debate of their day – any day. As long as we keep talking about machines, we can avoid talking about artmaking, and that would seem to be a good thing for a would-be artist who finds their soul a difficult thing to find or touch.

In the debate *du jour*, Adobe Photoshop is the devil (or our salvation). To the purists, digital imagery violates the truth of a photograph. So-called trick photography has been around since the invention of the camera. But, trick photographs have usually been very difficult to create and always somewhat detectable. The digital revolution in photography will eliminate both of these barriers. What will the response be – liberation or chaos? The debate rages and you are implored to engage it.

But, in my opinion, the real question is not who will win the debate – it is *how much creative time and energy will be lost by those who defend their chosen position*. In the end, it won't be logical or passionately persuasive arguments that carry the day – it will be won by those with the best, expressive, creative, visible and finely-crafted images – regardless of technique or technology.

Nonetheless, in the short term, the debate is quite vigorous and the arguments against digital tools mostly based in the "photography is truth" defense. Art Wolfe, for example, came under considerable fire for his digital manipulations in his book *Migrations* (Beyond Words Publishing, 1994). The cover image is a mass of running zebras, all tightly bunched together, filling the frame completely. The actual photograph, as recorded by the camera, is very, very close to the image in the book. However, there were a couple of places in the unmanipulated photograph that did not contain a zebra. For aesthetic reasons that had to do with artmaking, Wolfe elected to digitally copy and paste-in a few additional zebras to fill out the frame and create a photograph with more emotional impact. He hasn't done so surreptitiously. He confesses this digital manipulation without hesitation. So why has he come under such fire from his fellow nature photographers? Because supposedly, he lied. How ridiculous. I notice that he was never criticized for using a long telephoto lens that visually compresses the zebras closer to each other than they were in real life. I also assume that Wolfe's critics must actually believe that zebras are two dimensional and only a couple of inches tall.

Similarly, Bruce Barnbaum has been criticized for constructing a landscape from negatives photographed in two completely different areas. The resulting recombinant placed a series of sand dunes underneath a cliff – a scene which did not exist in reality. His defense was that this landscape could have existed at some point in time and that currently it existed in his mind's eye. His photograph was a constructed, believable fiction. It was also heresy to some.

The more important issue – personal expression in the creation of art –gets lost in these debates. Look at the history of art. Art was never intended to be a mere objective copy of nature. Iconographic paintings are *symbols*, not actual gods. Cave paintings of animals are not edible. Photographs of rivers are not wet. *What do they symbolize?* Works of art are symbols for ideas in our minds and emotions in our hearts. A work of art is a way to share these human, non-mechanical responses to our world with other people. A photograph of the Twin Towers means something to us now that is different than it meant on September 10th, 2001. Images are symbols for shared experiences. They either help us remember or teach us new ways of thinking or feeling.

Twenty-five (or a hundred) years from now, such discussions about photographic truthfulness will seem arcane and trite. They will seem so because photographers at that time will let go of their camera – the mechanical device that records *what is there* and more easily embrace a new tool – called a camera – which will certainly be different than those we have today, but will still be an image-capturing device. They will use these new cameras as artists do – to create what they see. Come to think of it, for those who are true artists, the future is now.

As photographers, we are so often embroiled in endless debates about technique and tools. This is all such a waste of time. Edward Weston made such wonderful photographs – in the most *primitive* darkroom I have ever seen. This same darkroom, by the way, would have seemed like a technological fantasy-come-true to photographers working fifty years earlier than *Pepper No. 30.* His tools are either primitive or advanced, depending on the point in time from which you examine them. His artwork, on the other hand, is timeless.

What is meaningful in art – in photography – is not the artifact or how it was produced. What makes a photograph meaningful is that it connects people to one another, connects our minds or our hearts in thought or emotion. Photography is not about grains of silver or pixels. It is not about pigments or machines, effort or ease. It is about you and what you want to say. It is about me and what you want me to see. It is ultimately about sharing – sharing life, sharing concerns, sharing triumph and sharing tragedy.

If you are interested in photography as an expressive art, the debates over cameras or techniques have probably been boring you for a long time. We had better get used to it – again. And, while the rest of the photographic world is debating truth vs. manipulation, pixels vs. chemistry, or film vs. memory storage, perhaps we can spend the next decade making images and artifacts that rise above the bickering about *how* one should be a photographer.

Twenty-one

A CHANGE OF VENUE

*There once a man who said "Damn,
for it seems that I certainly am
a creature who movesin determinant grooves.
I'm not even a bus. I'm a tram."*

We live in a world of yin and yang – the ever-opposing opposites: positive and negative, good and bad, up and down. If all things have their opposites, then what is the *opposite of creativity*? The answer is not obvious because there is more than one answer. But certainly, *one* possible opposite is *habit*.

Let me illustrate this with an exercise – you will need to play along. Count the number of *f*'s in the following phrase:

**Finished files are the final result
of years of scientific research.**

How many *f*'s did you count? If you haven't seen this before, there is an 85% chance, according to statistical odds, that you will have counted 4 *f*'s. If so, you are in good company or at least in the company of four-fifths of people who try this exercise. You are also wrong. There are 6 *f*'s. Try it again.

I use this puzzle to illustrate an important point about creativity: We don't see things as they *are*, but rather as we are *trained* to see them. My friend Morrie Camhi used to love to quote Anais Nin, "We don't see things as *they* are. We see things as *we* are." You see, because most of us are trained to read phonetically, we count the phonetic *f* sounds and tend not to see the *f*'s in the two words *of*. To our mind's eye these *f*'s are pronounced like the letter *v* and therefore, are skipped in the count. Most people skip them, not because they are illiterate, not because they are stupid and not because the letters are hidden. They are skipped because often we are ruled by our habits.

There is an old saw that says, "When your only tool is a hammer, the entire world looks like a nail." So it is with habits. Once engrained, they tend to change everything we see, everything we think we know, and – as addressed in this article – the way we create. Similarly, when your only tool is a specific kind of camera, the only things you will see to photograph are those things best suited to that camera.

I learned this lesson in a most tangible way, somewhat by accident. I purchased, for no particular reason, a new hand-held rangefinder. For over twenty years I had used only tripod-stabilized view cameras. Shortly after this purchase, I took a week's vacation on the Oregon coast where I intended to do some photography. Instead, I was weather-bound by a week of constant rain and wind. My spirits were as soggy as the landscape. Finally, on the last afternoon of the last full day, a break in the clouds delivered the most beautiful angular light across the beach at that soft and sculpting right-angle of winter. Seeing the beach dunes and grasses bathed in this amber glow, I knew my opportunity was fleeting. It was at this moment that I discovered the creative necessity of avoiding habits. I took a walk on the beach with my new camera and consequently, a new way of making photographs. I could not have predicted the effect – the experience changed the way I *see.*

First, my handheld camera gave me an incredible sense of freedom and fluidity; I was stunned by the flood of images that I started to see. Second, it allowed me to work more intuitively – reacting to the light and subject material without premeditation. Third, the camera allowed me to be so mobile that I found I simply *moved* more – up, then down, around the subjects, closer then farther away.

I had experienced the *yin* of the view camera, but had never worked with the *yang* of the handheld camera. Clearly both have their virtuous qualities: just like night and day. One is really no *better* than the other, but they are distinctly *different*. The question is which is *right* for the moment? When I owned the view camera only, such questions never occurred to me.

By nature, I tend to be conservative in my equipment and techniques. I have always believed that it was better to know a couple of films well than to skip all over the spectrum, never really exploring a set of variables deeply. I still believe in this and know that the best photography comes from those who thoroughly know their equipment and craft. The lesson I learned on the beach that day however, is that *habits* can be the opposite of creativity. Sometimes a change of venue: physical, mental, or equipment-oriented; a change in the medium; a change in the presentation, or a dozen other variables can be your most creative act. Habits are useful, but can easily become ruts. Shaking it up, from time to time, seems to be a good thing even though it might drive us, for a short period of time, out of our well-defined comfort zones.

There are habits of *thought*, too, just as there are habits of *action*. I've met so many photographers over the years who have thought the best photographs are made in the desert southwest, Yosemite or, more recently, Tibet or India. The habit of seeing our own neighborhood, culture, or geography makes photography at home difficult. We also tend to want to travel. But is photographing while we travel about seeing or about *us*?

Why are there so few great photographers from, say, the Midwest? (My apologies to David Plowden, Art Sinsabaugh, Harry Callahan, and, well, you know who you are.) Why are there no photographers of international acclaim from Winnipeg or Lubbock? Is there nothing to photograph there? I doubt it. I suspect the photographers from these places race off to Yosemite to photograph, forgetting that Ansel Adams lived in Yosemite for years!

Most photographers will agree that one of their most pressing problems is trying to determine *what* to photograph. It seems like such a simple task. In truth, like all the simple things in life, it takes a lifetime to get good at it. It is not necessary to travel to exotic locations to make visually stunning work. Learn to work close to home, to produce work in small spaces or short timeframes. The virtue of *access* outweighs any advantage that an exotic location might seem to offer.

More and more, I have come to think that examining *ourselves* is the true key to the creative life. Creativity – that overused word for such a mysterious process – is often simply the process of learning about ourselves, learning how we have placed limitations on our thinking, and finally, learning that we are our own barrier blocking the creative act. I am sure a psychologist somewhere would have a field-day with this statement but, as artists, it seems to be pragmatically true. Most often, a change of venue has nothing to do with a change in location, but everything to do with a change in the way we think.

Twenty-two

OWNING PHOTOGRAPHS

I remember when my kids were growing up, they both were enamored with the *Star Wars Trilogy.* They owned all three episodes on video tape and would watch each movie over and over *and over.* My Dad was always amazed at this because he could never understand why anybody would want to watch a movie a second time. "You know how it's going to end," he'd say to the kids with frustration. "Why do you want to watch it again?" To a small degree, I sympathized with his position, but I would remind him that he owned a number of LP's that he listened to frequently because he enjoyed hearing the music again and again, even though it was repetitive.

My kids watched those movies over and over again because they were fun – and they were fun every time they watched them. Similarly, my wife explains that she needs to listen to a new CD over and over until she "owns" the music – that is, until it is en-grained in her consciousness so well that she knows it intimately. But there is more going on here than mere repetitive appreciation or memorization.

Each time my kids watched *Star Wars,* the movie was the same – *they* were not. They'd changed, grown, seen other movies, learned, and added life experiences to bring to the movie the next time. This is the key. A good photograph, like a good movie or a good book or a good piece of music, *changes with you.* Every time I go back to one of my favorite books, *Tir 'a Mhurain* by Paul Strand, I see new things, different things; I see photographs I would swear I am seeing for the first time, even though I've read this book from cover to cover repeatedly over the years. At different times in my life, at different times of the year, at different moods, and even in different light, a good photograph offers a different experience, a changing experience.

We don't think this way anymore, in this day and age. We're supposed to "get it" quickly. We're supposed to get it *all* quickly. Flash, quick cut, boom, move on. Images are supposed to be disposable, like those little paper cups – one gulp and that's all there is to it. But isn't it axiomatic that things that are that easy are almost never the best choice? Fast food verses a home cooked meal, Cliff Notes verses the full Shakespearean text, guided tours verses wandering and discovering – there is supposedly a distillation in packaging, but it is far too often that the goods are over-boiled until the vitamins have been vaporized out of existence.

This is one of the problems of photography, in general. Photography itself is a distillation, a compression of experience into a reproduction that hangs on the wall so you can see it without having been there. Yet, if that's *all* photography is, we should destroy all the cameras and burn all the film. The good photographs, the ones that go beyond distillation, become gateways, candles, teachers, whacks on the head, friends, measures, reminders, and a compass. They cannot be all these things at once. It takes time and repetition for all of an image's qualities to emerge. A good photograph unfolds like a flower, not like a pop-up book.

Let me ask this question. The last time you looked at a photograph, how long did you look at it? My friend Morrie Camhi used to tell a story about an exercise he did with some of his photo students. Parked outside a photography gallery, they timed how long people spent inside, from the moment they entered the door to the moment they exited. The total time was then divided by the total number of photographs to calculate the average time spent per photograph. To their amazement, the average person spent just *2.7 seconds* per photograph.

Whenever I think of this story, I can't help but pity the poor photographer who sweated bullets to get the tone perfect only to have the audience glance at it with less focus than they do tying their shoes. The photographer would surely feel like they were cheated out of deserved attention, but in truth it's the audience who is cheated. They miss so much that the photographs have to offer, at least what the *good* photographs have to offer. Some might argue that an exhibition may not have any photographs worth spending much time but I can honestly say that I've *never* seen an exhibition without at least one photograph with something to offer. Well, okay, maybe I can think of one or two – but they're rare.

We can't control the audience and force them to look at our photographs – although the thought itself conjures up interesting ideas! As photographers, we must be pragmatic and practical about this issue. Most of the time, the audience has a relatively limited interest in what a photograph can offer. The key word in that sentence is *relatively* – they have a limited interest when *compared to the photograph's creator*. By analogy, you probably know less about the music you listen to than the composers, lyricists, and musicians who create and perform it. Their relationship to their artwork is deeper than yours. Similarly, your relationship to your photographs is deeper than that of your audience. This is only natural, and perhaps even as it should be. Each of us needs to be our own best audience. This is one of the best ways to become a better photographer.

Yet let's return to my original question: How long do *you* look at a photograph?

Let me propose an exercise. Take out a photograph you've made – any photograph will do – and prop it up so you can look at it from the comfort of a chair. Now sit down and start looking. While you're looking, observe *yourself* observing the photograph. How long did you look before you had the urge to move on? At what point did you think you'd "gotten it?"

Now expand the experiment just a bit. Write down, without using any pictures, the words that come to mind while you are looking at the photograph. Make two separate columns. The first column is for words that describe the photograph or the objects in the photograph. The second column is for words that describe *you* – your emotions, inferences you draw, associations you make, and, observations that might be unique to you and your life experiences invoked while observing the photograph. Don't stop until you have at least twenty-five words in each column.

If you are tempted to keep reading the article without doing the exercise, you might as well stop reading now. This exercise is not intended to be an *intellectual* one, but rather to show you something about yourself. If you wrote the fifty words, congratulations. If you didn't, it's not too late to do it now.

Now, take your piece of paper, fold it in half and staple it closed. Put the paper and the photograph away for six months. Schedule a time six months from now to pull out the photograph and a fresh piece of paper and repeat the exercise. Again, don't stop until you've written twenty-five words in each column. Then compare the two lists. What did you see the second time that you didn't see the first? What did you see the first time that you didn't see the second? How was the photograph changed? (This is a trick question.)

Here's another exercise courtesy of Ray McSavaney. He used this exercise in a workshop I took in 1981 and it changed my photography profoundly. For this exercise, choose from memory – *and without looking at it* – one of your favorite photographs. It should be a photograph you've made. Now, draw a sketch of the photograph, putting in all of the lines and graphical elements of the photograph. Don't worry if you can't sketch worth beans, a rough "stick figure" representation of the photograph will be good enough for our purposes.

When you've completed the sketch, pull out the photograph and compare your sketch to the photograph. What did you leave out? What did you put in that's not there in the original photograph? What is it that you see in your mind's eye that an audience will see differently, or not at all?

One of the chief reasons I love this exercise is because it teaches this simple principle; it's not that repeated viewing allows us to see more, but sometimes, it helps us to see *less*. That is to say, sometimes repeated viewing distills the image in our mind's eye to the important elements and we mentally exclude the unimportant elements that our audience will not be able to ignore.

This is one of the chief reasons to own photographs – you will both see more and see less with the passage of time. Try this exercise again, but this time with a photograph made by someone else. When you've completed your sketch, don't look at the photograph for a few days. Then, a week or so later, pull out the photograph (or the book) and look at the photograph closely. Really take some time to see it deeply. Then put the image away, out of sight, and immediately make another sketch of it. When this second sketch is complete, pull out the first sketch and compare it to the second one. Then, compare both of them to the original image. I've done this exercise a number of times and it never fails to teach me about seeing.

In fact, I've become fascinated with variations to this exercise. Try it with different photographers. Whose images do you remember most accurately? Try it with different media. What is the difference between color photographs and black and white ones? Try it with printing variations of an image you are currently working on. Does the higher contrast version "read" better than the soft contrast one?

Oliver Gagliani told me a story about purchasing a violin as a youngster. He and his father went to buy a violin and they couldn't decide between two; they both looked good and sounded fine. Finally, they devised this test: they took the two violins out into a field and played each one while they walked farther and farther apart until one of the violins demonstrated that it could clearly "carry" the sound farther than the other. He told me this story in response to the question I asked about why he used Agfa Multigrade paper instead of the other brands. He took me down to his print finishing room and put up two photographs made from the same negative but printed on different papers. As we backed up, step by step, viewing the two photographs from an increasing distance, the one printed on Agfa "held up" while the other started to pale in comparison. It was a fascinating experiment.

This led me to yet another variation on my "sketch" exercise. Try it from different distances! There is nothing revolutionary here and the results are somewhat predictable. What was startling was that I had never thought of it when actually printing in my darkroom. What differences are demanded when the photograph will be seen only from a distance or only up close? Paul Strand used to print for a specific illumination. Some photographers insist that each image be made only in one size. Hmmm . . .

The point of all this fuss is simply this, if I may paraphrase G.K. Chesterton: "It's amazing how many things there *are*, that *aren't so*." The minute I *know* what a photograph looks like, I know I'm in trouble. The only intelligent way to approach viewing a photograph is to remain open to the possibility that it may be different the next time I see it. To quote Anais Nin, "We see things not as *they* are. We see them as *we* are." This is true both as a photographer and as a viewer.

Twenty-three

WHEN IT BECOMES
A PROJECT

When I was a bit younger, I used to spend as much time as possible backpacking and hiking the trails of the great Pacific Northwest. I spent almost every weekend of the summer engaged in an outing in which the primary activity was to "beat feet." I don't do it anymore and a friend of mine recently asked me why. I offered the predictable excuses – I don't have any time, my priorities have changed, I'm too old. Of course, all these excuses are just that – excuses. The truth is much more subtle.

I remember my first backpacking experience clearly. It was an impromptu affair suggested by a friend, late one Friday afternoon. Ill-equipped, ill-prepared, ill-trained, and ill-advised, we headed out to the woods to barely sleep two nights, eat badly, get wet, and have more fun than I'd had in years. The next trip, I decided it would be even *more* fun if I was slightly more pre-pared. As the weekends rolled by and my experience increased, my equipment demands increased as well. Pretty soon what was a tennis-shoes-and-matchbook affair turned into hiking boots, Thinsulate sleeping bags, rip-stop nylon tents, freeze-dried food, and more-and-more sophisticated and expensive equipment. Impromptu fun changed to planned outings, which changed to highly organized adventures, which changed to projects with goals and objectives, and higher and higher stakes. What start-ed off as a romp in the forest had become an endurance trek in the wilderness. What had started out as a fun activity had developed into an intense and serious project. In the process, I squashed the fun right out of the woods.

I hadn't realized what I'd done to this delightful experience until another friend mentioned how often he had noticed this pattern in other areas of life. Engage anything seriously, he proposed, and quickly it will seduce you into "gearing up." There are experts to learn from, equipment to buy, skills to be learned, and progress to be made. This applies to any hobby you can think of – golf, hunting, skiing, stamp collecting, cooking, furniture making – there is an industry of people waiting to outfit you, educate you, and turn your lark into a project of major proportions and, in turn, make it work.

The minute you turn something into a *project* it becomes fundamentally different than *play*. I've found this a great lesson in my life, particularly when applied to photography. The natural seduction in photography is to pursue larger and larger projects requiring ever-more sophisticated levels of craft, complexity, expense, and equipment. That's why, from time-to-time, I purposely remind myself that the reason I'm doing photography is for *fun*.

Another friend who moved from Arkansas to Oregon found that he was spending more and more time locked-up in the office at his business. Work begot work, until finally, in frustration, he posted signs all over his house, his office, and his car that said – *Remember why you moved to Oregon*. He now spends more time fishing.

I see a consistent theme repeated at workshops. One after another, people drag out their portfolios, lay the work out to be seen by all, and then proceed to describe *how long they have been working on this project*. *Months* are rare, *years* are more common. I've done this myself. It's as though there is some virtue in how long one has taken to complete a project, and – based on the pride these people exhibit when describing the turmoil of producing their portfolio – that there is a link between the value of the project and the length of time to produce it. If someone happens to show a body of work and then confess that they "whipped it out in a couple of hours one Saturday afternoon" the work is too easily dismissed as somehow trivial and shallow – simply because it was relatively easy and did not require Herculean efforts to complete.

I've often speculated that this bragging about *turmoil* is somehow connected with the guilt that photographers feel because they can produce a significant piece of artwork in 1/60th of a second. Real artists – primarily painters and sculptors – toil for long hours to produce a piece of artwork. Photographers, on the other hand, can just fire away – click – it's art! At least that's the prevailing myth that even photographers feel on a subconscious level.

We need not feel guilty for the technical ease of our craft. The old cliché is true – machines don't make photographs. What about the years of practice? What about the tens of thousands of exposures that have helped develop the artistic eye? What about the hours and hours spent wandering the countryside? Playing with studio set-ups? Looking at photographs? Thinking about photographs? The time, expense, and hassle of every technical test from Zone System development to the effects of shutter speed blur? Don't all these experiences also accumulate and count in that fleeting 1/60th of a second that makes that piece of artwork? Is it necessary that one spends hours, or even decades, developing a body of work? Clearly, sometimes it is, but this should not invalidate the simpler project – the easier project – the pleasant afternoon that generates, almost without effort, a sweet little portfolio of a dozen prints. If other disciplines can talk about the "flash of insight" why can't photography have (no pun intended) a flash of insight that generates a significant photographic product in a short period of time?

How long did it take Paul Strand to photograph *Tir a' Mhurain*? How long did it take Michael Kenna to photograph the images for his book *The Elkhorn Slough*? The final work doesn't give us any clues. Do we care? *Should* we care? Wright Morris produced three seminal photography books – *The Inhabitants, Home Place,* and *God's Country and My People* – with photographs he made during a few weeks of intense photographing. Obviously, the image of the artist as a struggling, long-suffering, patient, and dedicated producer is often nothing more than a handsome myth.

Imogen Cunningham once said that if you were a decent photographer you could make a significant piece of artwork in your own backyard. She may have meant this literally, but she could have meant it figuratively just as well. There are great photographs to be made outside of the streets of New York City, the villages of Tibet, Yosemite, or Point Lobos and other locations so commonly the destination of photographers looking for artistic and photogenic subject material. The primary requirement to produce an interesting portfolio of work is *not* a pile of money and unlimited time or travel – but rather, a definitive passion, a sufficient commitment, and a clear understanding that when producing artwork *effort* and *quality* do not directly equate.

Twenty-four

WORK & PLAY

Play, *from the Anglo Saxon word* plegan
and the Middle Dutch word pleyen
meaning "to bestir one's self, to rejoice, to dance"

I remember an assignment from my high school chemistry class that consisted of one instruction – "Observe a pencil." We were to write a list of everything we could see, measure and otherwise observe about a standard, yellow #2 pencil. How boring. How stupid. How idiotic to waste my time with such an assignment.

I endured a dozen or so such observations – using brilliant comments like "It is yellow" and "It is smaller than a bread box" – until I thought I would die from the boredom. Finally, I complained to my teacher and he replied, "You are making this assignment into work. Just play with it!" The word struck me with force – you are making this into *work*. He stated it as if I had a choice.

Work is a negative, prejudiced-laden word. We go to work, we work at it, work it out, work around it, work our fingers to the bone, work our butts off, and become workaholics. Conversely, we play around, laugh and play, play instruments and games, entertain ourselves at the playground, and go to a play. We are against work and in favor of play. The dichotomy is one of absolute opposites.

In fact, I've noticed over the years that most people divide their lives between work and play, and complain there is far too much of the former and not enough of the latter. We want more vacation days and a shorter work week.

And then there are artists. Artists seem to have the uncanny knack of making work into play – a strategy that serves them very well. I was recently showing a new portfolio to a non-artist who commented, with a certain amount of disdain, that "that must have been a lot of work." Their tone communicated clearly that they considered work and anything associated with work to be dreary and avoided, if possible. They seemed incredulous that I would engage the work of making art with enthusiasm – and on a voluntary basis. This led me to consider a question: Is the artist's perspective one that combines work and play into one activity? One of insight and creative union or one of masochistic self-sacrifice? Or both?

To do your art is to "do your work." An artist's relationship with play and work is unusual. It is often said that creating art is 1% inspiration and 99% perspiration. The implication is that it is 1% play and 99% work – necessary work that must be grunted through, whether we like it or not. I've noticed, however, this is not the case. Most photographers seem to derive some sense of enjoyment from the darkroom or the computer. Most painters seem to like mixing paint. In fact, most artists experience a letdown at the end of a project. It is not a *relief* to be finished, but a *disappointment.*

In general, artists both crave and love the work. They may also crave and *loathe* it, too. Dorothy Parker, for example, once said, "I hate to write, but love to have written."

The best artists, however, seem to be able to play while working and work while playing. The fusion of the discipline of work with the volunteerism of play is the key. If two people have the same objective and one is motivated by fun and one dreads the project, their results will be clearly different and are bound to demonstrate their feelings toward the project. This is just simple human nature.

For me, making work into play is a magic that has added incalculable value to my life. Zen Master Shunryu Suzuki said, "If the spirit of repetition leaves you, your work will become difficult." I may not always remember this advice when developing my fortieth roll of film, but when I do, it helps.

The importance of this concept became clear to me during

a conversation with a friend. He had not produced any new work for several years. I asked him about this lack of work and he replied that it just took too much work to get out there and shoot, develop film, print, mat, frame and show. He is right, of course. The rewards are far too small for anyone to pursue the creation of art as a means of barter for goods or happiness. If this is true, there are only two reasons to pursue the path of an artist – it is either a neurosis or it is fun.

There is another aspect of work and play that has fascinated me for years. Work tends to be associated with business. In business, the objective is generally to make something that will satisfy the customer yet to make it with the least cost and effort. Any additional cost or effort is "overproducing" and wasteful. On the other hand, we make art regardless of the cost and effort required and will expend any amount of time, energy, and resources to pursue perfection – regardless of the customer, if any, or their wishes. Business (as most people practice it) tends to minimize quality and maximize profit. Art (as most people practice it) tends to maximize quality but profit, well, is simply not in the equation.

These divisions are not *necessary* definitions of either business or art, but have become prevalent distinctions in our culture. Business can be the pursuit of quality (I like to think that *LensWork* is an example of this) and art can be a profitable pursuit (think Thomas Kinkade or Bev Doolittle). When reading that last sentence, did you flinch at all? In art circles, Thomas Kinkade and Bev Doolittle are common examples of sell-outs, hacks, and commercial phonies whose art is somehow tainted precisely because it is commercially successful. Despite their widespread mainstream appeal, their work is not respected in fine art circles. Why? Is it because their work is trite, or because they have merged work and play so completely? They both get paid – handsomely, I might add – for playing. It seems to me that this is an admirable strategy.

As a habit of thought, the division between work and play is even more instructive. I've noticed another consistency: The best artists tend to carry their devotion to quality into other areas of their lives as well. The pursuit of excellence influences their non-art activities. They are often excellent cooks or superb gardeners, for example. This is usually attributed to their manual dexterity or their eye for aesthetics. I think it is more convincing that artists who value play and the pursuit of quality at any cost, bring this attitude to all areas of their life. They would rather have a well-cooked meal than a fast one, a garden of delights than an expanse of lawn – and the time to create is less troublesome to them than the punishment of fast food or of mowing the lawn.

Another friend suggested this approach: When faced with any challenge (whether work or play) he asks himself the question, "How far can I take this game?" I use his question often. For example, how *much* grain can I get into a print? How *little* grain can I get? How far can I take a negative before the printing changes I make are so subtle that no one will ever see them? How much emotion can I get into a portrait? In essence, where is the limit? Of course, there is never a limit. In essence, the pursuit of limits can dissolve work into a delightful romp. Art is not just a matter of creation, but of discovering the absence of limits to creation. It has often been said that "art is all about edges" and adds another edge to the discussion.

All of this may seem rather simplistic, but I believe these examples demonstrate a powerful and universal principle: Work and play are not separate parts of an activity; they are frames of mind. Cleaning the garage can be work, if you dread it. It can be play, if you view it as a game. As work, cleaning the garage is definitely boring. As play, cleaning the garage is a game and a chance to pursue quality and aesthetics – it is an extension of our art. You might laugh, but it is true.

I've tested this principle for over twenty years and can report that anything – *anything* – can be turned into a game of fun. Simply ask, "How well can I do this?" On an artist's creative path, one of the great lessons is that artmaking is not a division of life, but is life itself – or at least it can be. It is when we choose to allow this philosophy to guide our thoughts, we can realize the power of artmaking. When this fusion transforms us, the difference between work and play dissolves and the only word left to describe what you do is *art*. This fusion is a likely explanation for the phrases the *cooking arts* or the *martial arts*. When asked recently for my definition of the word *artist*, I replied "a person who pursues excellence as a way of life."

Art is not something that we do outside of life. It *is* our life, and has the power to engulf every activity. The more the spirit of art infuses you, the more you find the wonder of possibilities and opportunities for continual play in life. What you do becomes less important than your attitude. The more we look at life as the pursuit of excellence, the more it becomes play, and the more that play becomes an extension of our art.

Twenty-five

How Old is Too Old?

It is not very significant or insightful to say that our culture values youth above nearly all other virtues. Baseball pitcher Nolan Ryan is a once-in-a-century anomaly whose professional athletic career extended well into his aged forties. Typically, a thirty-five-year-old athlete is washed up. The media sells youth and popularity as a linked pair and suggests that we are at our best when at the peak of our youth.

A friend of mine, Washington photographer David Grant Best, turned forty a few years ago. At the age of 35, he quit his "day job," took up the camera full-time and embarked on his serious photographic career. At that point, he was in the full flush of youth, but edging into middle age.

When he turned forty, he told me he was feeling pressure. In the five years he had been a full-time artist, he felt he hadn't produced anything of significance nor done anything to further his career other than simply photograph and produce lots of negatives. He had not published a book. He had not exhibited in a major show. He was, in short, distressed that his career seemed stalled and, that now he was getting older, he might have lost some of his opportunity.

He restated this lament when he turned forty-one and again when he turned forty-two (in spite of releasing his first book of photographs, *Portrait of a Racetrack*, a few days before his birthday).

In essence, David posed a fascinating question: If an athlete is washed-up at 35, when is a photographer washed-up? (No pun intended.) I began an informal survey to see if I could answer that question.

In my survey, I asked, "At what age did the well-known photographers produce their well-known works?" In the data I gathered, I included the dates they made the negatives of their great works, the publication of portfolios, major exhibitions and book publication dates. My survey was both enlightening and encouraging.

Ansel Adams at 42

When Ansel Adams was 42, the same age as my friend, he was just photographing *Clearing Winter Storm*. He was four years away from photographing *Oak Tree, Snowstorm*, and *Tenaya Creek, Dogwood, Rain* and four years from producing his *Portfolio No. 1*. At the age of 42, he had photographed *Moonrise, Hernandez* just two years earlier. *Portfolio No. 2* was six years into his future. Both versions of his famous aspen photographs were 14 years away and it would take him another 16 years to produce *Moon and Halfdome* and *Portfolio No. 3*. He wouldn't do *Portfolio No. 4* until he was 61, *No. 5* until he was 68, *No. 6* until he was 72 and *Portfolio No. 7* until he was 74!

Paul Strand at 42

At age 42, Paul Strand was eight years from publishing the Mexican Portfolio and wouldn't begin photographing for his classic book, *Time in New England*, for another 12 years. He wouldn't publish *Un Paese* for 23 years and *Tir 'a Mhurain* was still 30 years away!

Edward Weston at 42

At age 42, Edward Weston had just completed the shell pictures, was two years away from doing *Pepper No. 30*, nine years from photographing the *Surf at Orick* and would not receive his Guggenheim Grant and start the photography for his classic book, *California and the West*, for 12 more years.

In fact, look closely at the notable *lack* of images these people made in their twenties. The single exception to the rule is Adams' *Monolith, Face of Half Dome*. In fact, few of these notable artists made important or memorable images in their thirties whereas the forties and fifties seem to be universally the decades of fruition for most photographic artists.

It's also fascinating to note that in their biographies, almost without exception, famous photographers began their careers in their early twenties. A quick bit of math shows conclusive evidence that many of these individuals spent 15 years or more just developing their craft, their eye, their sensitivity, and their maturity. In most cases, they didn't produce their greatest work until they'd been "at it" regularly – one suspects almost daily – for twenty, thirty or forty years.

I think it is also important to note that Ansel Adams' great fame – certainly the greatest of all photographers – didn't skyrocket until the late 1960s and early '70s, when he was in his late sixties. In 1974, when Ansel was 72 years old, the vast majority of his work could still be purchased for a few hundred dollars.

Why is it that our generation insists that success must come so early in life? Is it impatience, the desire for instant gratification, the lack of long-term discipline or the speed at which our world is now changing? I have often felt that many of the young photographers whose work I have seen exhibited, should have waited to exhibit for a while longer and instead continued to work. This is not to say that their work was bad, only that perhaps their best work was still ahead. Why try to establish a reputation and career on work that is not fully developed, not their best, possibly "student work," derivative, or work that demonstrates an immature vision?

Fame is seductive. And, of course, moneys follows – and even sometimes chases – fame. More money makes travel and photography more possible. It's no wonder that, with this paradigm, so many photographers are in a race to establish their careers in their youth.

But, it goes deeper. Rather than let the work speak for itself, artists often try to use their work to build their career, as if their career is more important than the work. This shift in priority seems to indicate their focus lies in building a career, rather than in creating the work that composes it.

My friend's lament that his career was going nowhere was understandable, but highly inaccurate. During his thirties, he may not have been publishing, exhibiting or famous, but he was working hard, working daily, working with diligence at the true task of an artist – seeing, learning, feeling, responding. He was producing work: photographing and producing negatives. Perhaps, if the lives of the masters of the craft are a good model, he was accurately focused for his age and his stage in a photographic career.

There is no other substitute for the virtues of experience and the production of thousands of images. It is almost a rule without exception that young photographers who exhibit too early, in their twenties or thirties, burn-out producing financially unrewarding, derivative or even clone images just about the time they develop their own vision. In the last 30 years, I have seen it happen often.

There are tragedies in life that can cut a career short and a variety of turns in life that can divert it. There is, however, no shortcut to the learning process. In our youth-oriented culture, photography is a naturally techno-driven, hip art. It appeals to those who are energetic and driven. This is nowhere more true than in digital photography, where the hybrid of images and computers seem to be a perfect combination for a young, quick mind. However, all of these statements say more about technology than about art. Artmaking, the true core of an artist's life, is only peripherally involved in technology. Artmaking is a matter of the soul, a matter only deeply explored when the artist has enough life experience to face mortality. Sure, great art can and is created by people of all ages, but there is a distinct advantage when experience informs your work. It is no accident that so many of the great photographers' best work was made late in their lives. As it turns out, feeling and experience are the most important tools in photography.

Twenty-six

WHAT IS YOUR
NATURAL VISION?

I tend to avoid sports analogies in my writing, but I'd like to make an exception here. I *love* baseball's designated hitter rule. Let me explain: The designated hitter rule states that the pitcher – all pitchers are notoriously bad batsman – does not take his turn at bat in the normal rotation. Instead, the *designated hitter* bats in his place. This player has one task in life, a task at which they often excel, and that's simply to hit. They don't play the outfield. They don't pitch. Often, they don't even run. A hitter is a hitting expert and his purpose is to make the game more exciting by adding extra hitting and offense. I think this a splendid idea.

You may be asking what this has to do with photography. It's simply this: my experience has shown that there is great wisdom in acknowledging the specialist. Just as in baseball, not every photographer is equally talented at all kinds of photography. In fact, I'd go so far as to say that most photographers truly excel at only a few kinds of imagery. Ansel Adams was a superb black and white landscape photographer. His efforts with color photography are questionable. Arnold Newman does portraits beautifully, but his grand landscapes, are . . . well . . . did I mention how well he does portraits? He is a specialist, as is Ansel Adams, as are most great photographers. They are photography's equivalent of the designated hitter and, I believe, to their credit and photography's benefit.

What I find so curious is *how* we tend to define our specialties. I recently attended a gallery opening where the photographer's brochure announced that she was a "Large Format, Black & White, Photographer." I found this definition incredibly odd! She defined herself by a certain kind of equipment. Would writers define themselves as a "word processorist," a "typewriterist," or a "pencil-and-paperist?"

You see, the question is not your equipment or even your subject material. What really counts is *how* you see, *what* you see, and what you *say* when you see. Let me illustrate this with three specific photographers as examples – I'll start with myself.

Several years ago, I was showing my work to a friend, a fine photographer. As we were talking about my photographs, she made a rather startling observation of my work – an observation which was new to me, quite shocking, and as I thought about it more deeply, absolutely correct. She noticed that all of my photographs could easily be divided into two piles, the ones that succeeded and the ones that didn't – not too unusual for a photographer. But, she also noticed the second pile were all my grand landscapes! The more we talked about it the more I came to realize that she was absolutely correct – the grand landscape is not one of my strong suits.

On the other hand, she showed me that almost all of my best photographic work involved subject material that fell in the range between two and 15 feet from my camera – regardless if it was landscape. Before this analysis, I tended to see (and define) myself as a landscape photographer. She saw me as a photographer with an eye for a certain type of object, with a certain scale, at a certain distance, with a certain inter-relationship in 3-dimensions. Once she pointed this out to me, I started concentrating on subject material in that range of distances from the camera. Much to my surprise, my photography improved dramatically, instantly. For reasons I don't understand, I tend to see in that range; I don't know why; I can't explain it. I don't know if it is psychological or physical, I just know that it is so. Knowing this about myself has radically altered my approach to subject material, products, equipment, and methods. I've become a specialist.

This is not to say that I *can't* photograph the grand landscape.

It's equally unfair to say that a baseball pitcher can't hit a baseball. I can and he can. For both of us, knowing our natural limitations and our natural talents is an asset that can be consciously exploited – or consciously avoided.

This doesn't mean, by the way, that I no longer photograph the grand landscape. It does mean, however, that I am much more cautious and careful because I know my instincts in the grand landscape are suspect. When working with subject material that is within my "photographic sweet spot," I find I can trust my instinct and intuition with greater regularity and confidence. This may not be knowledge that alters my subject material, but it is knowledge – important, self-evaluative, honest knowledge – that has the potential to make my images stronger.

I've discussed this idea with another photographer who is a friend of mine. In a similar exercise, we examined his body of work to try to find his natural vision. Again, as in the case of my own photography, we found that his natural vision was not limited to a subject matter, methodology, or even scale. In his case, his best images all contained an incredible panoply of detail. Bald skies are not his forté. Detailed undergrowth, desert southwest rock fields, and other subjects where the presentation of minutia in relationship to one another best defines the way he sees. In his case, his natural vision favors the view camera, even the 8x10 over the 4x5. Does this mean he can't be successful making photographs with medium format or 35 mm? No, in fact he's made some wonderful photographs with all these formats. It's not that he can't, it's just that he has to work a little harder at photographing with the small films. Of even more interest was that his photographs using the 8x10 camera that *don't* show exquisite detail and patterns of minutia tend, generally, to be not as strong as those that do. Here again, its not equipment that defines his vision, but vision that defines his equipment.

The third photographer I'll mention – Larry Wiese – has a natural vision that is defined by a certain visual style. Larry tells the story of making and presenting his work to a gallery owner in the hopes of gaining representation and an exhibition.

Part way through the presentation of his portfolio, he suddenly broke into a cold sweat and had an anxiety attack that was so strong that he interrupted his presentation halfway through, apologized and retreated. His strong reaction when presenting his work bothered him for some time and fueled a great deal of introspection. Finally, he saw that the source of his anxiety was the realization that the work he'd been presenting to the gallery owner was *not his own vision.* He had been mimicking, up to that point, someone else's eye – their style and their vision.

In the subsequent months, he began from scratch. He changed his camera, his darkroom technique, everything about his vision. Through a series of lengthy experiments and explorations, tests and retreats, questions and more questions, with precision and hard work, he eventually found a visual style that he feels exactly represents his internal vision. His images now tend to be printed quite dark, yet full of light. They are heavily diffused, showing shapes without details. They present emotions, even moods, in archetype references. He prints on matte paper and achieves an inky, sensual surface with his prints that is exquisite. *This* is his vision, not the hard-edged, razor-sharp, zone-and-tone work of the West Coast landscape that characterized his earlier images.

Once Larry found the style of his natural vision, his creative output increased explosively. Forget the old adage about ten good prints defining a great photographic year. Larry often creates ten great prints in just a few rolls of film! The volume of his work in the last five or six years is staggering. He will admit he doesn't know how long this creative vision will flow so easily, but it is fascinating to watch him work with ease and brilliance now that he is in sync with his natural vision.

By the way, Larry recently showed me some of his early, traditional, tack-sharp, classic West Coast imagery. It was excellent. He knows how to print, knows his way around the Zone System, and can produce this type of work when necessary. What makes his creative path so interesting is that he, like so many others who have described a similar catharsis, had to work *through* the vision of those who went before him before he found his own vision. Picasso could paint a classic Renaissance scene, but moved beyond that vision to find his own in cubist representations. Similarly, Larry Wiese understands and values the traditions that have gone before him, but extends that tradition into his own creative vision.

In these three examples, each of us found a way to specialize our creative work to synchronize with our natural vision. We came to recognize that we were naturally predisposed to see in some ways more strongly than in others. By knowing this, we could more easily know when it might be best to work intuitively and when it might be best to work more intellectually or carefully.

It is not necessary or even recommended that you work exclusively in a given style or with a given subject even if it is your natural vision. Such pigeon-holing can be stifling and oppressive. However, a solid understanding of your natural talent is a useful tool in developing a strategy for success. Pitchers may have fun swinging the bat and there is nothing wrong with having fun, but they probably shouldn't focus their career on a talent that is not their strongest. Letting the pitchers pitch and the designated hitters hit makes both of them more successful.

So, the question is, what do *you* see? What is your natural vision?

Twenty-seven

WHY I AM NOT A PHOTOGRAPHER

Gather together a half dozen photographers and start a conversation about photography and its place in the Arts. The group will quickly, and sometimes emotionally, divide into two distinct camps.

There are those who will claim that photographic art is produced by the "artsy-fartsy crowd" who can't make a decent image and whose pursuit of art is replete with arrogant elitism. This camp will also uphold salability and appreciation by the masses as the virtuous yardstick to judge the value of a photograph.

The other camp will, with considerable indignation, accuse the first camp of being "mere hacks." They will claim that photography for the masses is mere calendar art and a debasement of photography's true artistic potential. If the conversation proceeds long enough, a member of the second camp will probably quote George Bernard Shaw, "If more than 10% of the people appreciate your art, you can be assured that it is shallow, trivial and worthless." (That's not exactly what he said, but it is often the form the quotation takes!) The second camp delights in the esoteric. The first camp delights in broad appeal.

That these two opposing views exist is not surprising. That these two philosophies should be so *antagonistic* toward one another is surprising. The confusion arises, in my opinion, because of a simple lack of definition of terms.

Photography is nothing more than a means of communication. It is a language and often referred to with the cliché "visual language." It is a means of expressing ideas, of communicating, of formulating a thought and sharing it, telling it or yelling it. If you would review that last sentence you would see that this exact same definition could apply to the written word. Writing is a form of communication. The parallels between writing and photography can be instructive.

If you have an opportunity ask a local newspaper writer what they do for a living. He will likely respond, "I'm a journalist." Ask someone who writes poems for a living or in their free time what they are. They'll proudly announce that they are a poet. Ask someone who creates restaurant menus, billboard signs, advertising inducements, corporate memos, prescription labels, term paper, or other forms of the written word what they do and you will likely *never* hear "I am a writer." In fact, if I announce to you that "I am a writer," what image comes to mind? Most likely you will think I am a novelist and rarely would you suspect that I write, say, song lyrics.

Writing is a sophisticated form of communication. Its history spans a couple of centuries. Its forms are well defined, well understood and infrequently confused. The terminology that has surrounded those who write provides precise definitions for describing each type of writing. Photography, on the other hand, has been a part of history now less than 200 years. Its uses, definitions, perceptions, and visual history are still beginning to be defined.

This adolescent maturity leads to considerable confusion. Take the example of an individual who derives their living by creating commercial advertising photographs. Ask this person what they do for a living and their response will be, "I am a photographer." Ask the person who takes family pictures of you and your loved one in the professional studio what they are and the answer will be, "I am a photographer." Ask a person who take pictures for publication in the daily newspaper — "I am a photographer." The individual who uses cameras and lenses to create works of art for galleries and museums — "I am a photographer." All these uses of the medium of photography are lumped together in language *and in thought* under the generalized term *photography*.

This is why, when I confess that I am a photographer, strangers advise me to go up to the local mountain pass where I can get some fantastic photos of the pristine mountain lakes, alpine sunsets and the wild grizzly bears. Those who offer such advice don't understand the difference between their perception of photographic art and my interests (which lean toward Edward Weston/Walker Evans/Paul Strand/Lewis Hine/Wright Morris). I sometimes cringe and hesitate to even tell people that I am a photographer because I know what they think of when I use the term. What they think is not *at all* what I mean. In fact, I don't even *own* a motordrive.

Few people, even among the "bowling and beer" crowd wouldn't confuse the writing of Charles Dickens and Carl Sandberg, let alone lump them together in the same group. But tell them you are a photographer and watch out!

Several years ago, I took a vacation with a group of friends, none of whom were photographers. You can imagine my dismay when I learned that not one person on the trip had brought a snapshot camera because they all assumed that I, with my monorail and tripod, would serve as the group's photographer. They assumed that I would happily make reprints available to them in far superior quality than they could achieve with their little pocket cameras. You can imagine their dismay when they learned that all I had with me was black and white film. I enthusiastically accepted their assignment and proceeded to make the first photograph of the outing. Setting up the tripod, assembling my collapsible camera, taking meter readings, focusing under the dark cloth, *et al* required 40 minutes or so. At least I *made* it require 40 minutes. Funny, every time I mentioned that this might be a good spot for another photograph, they quickly disappeared. The opening group portrait was the only picture of the entire vacation.

The core idea of this article is simply that *words have meaning*. It behooves us to understand the meaning of words when we use them; yet, here is the problem: the word *photographer* means something to non-photographers that it does not mean to photographers. In the same way, the term *imaginary number* means something to a mathematician that is quite different than the concept we non-mathematicians might entertain.

When I realized this several years ago, I changed my letterhead and my business card stationery. I removed all occurrences of the word photographer. My stationery now says *Brooks Jensen Arts*. Although my work is primarily *photographic* arts, the word artist conveys to the general public much more accurately *what I do* than the word *photographer*. When we understand the words *as they are heard*, we can communicate more effectively.

I am therefore proposing that we photographers follow the lead of the novelist, the poet, journalist and the copywriter. When someone asks what you do, answer that you are a portaitist, a landscapist, a studio constuctionist, an advertising imagist, or a weddingist.

Come to think of it, maybe *photographer* isn't such a bad term after all.

Twenty-eight

THINGS I'VE LEARNED ABOUT PHOTOGRAPHY

It's been 34 years since I developed my first roll of film in junior high school. There is not a day that goes by that I don't think about or do photography. Certainly, in all that time I must have learned something of value! What follows are tidbits that I've learned about photography from direct experience. They are personal, experiential and may not be true for everyone. Yet perhaps they will stimulate thought and as such, be of value – or a laugh!

This list is composed of some original thoughts mixed with some thoughts I think are original (but undoubtedly are not) because I've forgotten where and from whom I first learned them. There are also a few whose author I am delighted to thank and credit. To those named and unnamed sources, I ask for some creative license if I don't remember the quotation exactly. Where I quote another, I do so because I have found their wisdom true in my own experience; they've expressed it better than I can. The list is not composed of any particular order.

- Finding great subject matter is an art in itself.
- Good lenses and cameras are worth the price.
- Your success depends as much upon the viewer as it does on you.
- A lazy photographer dies before he makes many photographs.
- Most people see good pictures and photograph bad ones. Real photography begins when we let go of what we have

been told is a good photograph and start photographing what
we see.

- Some things just can't be photographed. Trying to do so
  anyway is still worthwhile.
- Photographers are more scared of people than people are of
  photographers.
- Don't be afraid of rain. Cameras can get a lot wetter than you
  might guess.
- It takes a lot of practice to learn how to see what makes a good
  photograph better than a bad one.
- For the first several years, you struggle with technical
  challenges, making sure and steady progress; you experience
  a rewarding learning curve and grow in a process that is
  rewarding, stimulating and self-renewing. But eventually,
  every photographer who sticks with it long enough arrives
  at a technical plateau where production of a technically good
  photograph is relatively easy. Real photography begins at this
  nexus and once they arrive at this plateau, most photographers
  quit.
- Working photographers rarely die of consumption.
- If you believe in regular habits, don't take up photography.
- Books on photography offer little of help.
- You can do everything right and still fail.
- Emotions are more important than details.
- "There is nothing worse than a sharp photograph of a fuzzy idea."
  Ansel Adams
- "The best people make the best photographs." *Morley Baer*
- The scarier it is to make a photograph, the more you are likely
  to learn from doing it.
- There is no such thing as "good" or "bad" photographic light.
  There is just light.
- "The least valuable thing you can tell another photographer is
  that you either like or dislike their photograph." *David Bayles*
- Breaking the rules is one of the greatest sources of growth
  and will always result in lots of criticism from the small-
  minded.

- Breaking the rules does not ensure you will achieve anything of value; you will not necessarily learn anything or make a good photograph. Sometimes the small-minded are right.
- If you want to sell a lot of photographs, use *lots* of color. If you want to sell even more, photograph mountains, oceans, fall leaves, and animals.
- Photography, too, is 1% inspiration and 99% perspiration.
- If you are even the least bit tempted, make the photograph now! The subject will not be the same later.
- If you are not in the least bit tempted now, don't block the subject from your mind as a future possibility. All things change.
- The second, third and fourth time you photograph something, will produce more refined compositions than the first time. These may or may not be better photographs. You will never know, however, unless you make the second, third and fourth photographs.
- Getting closer to the subject improves 98% of all photographs. Telephoto lenses are not the answer.
- Duracell and Kodak financed the research and development of the motor drive. Very few photographers, with the exception of sports photographers, need one. They sure do sound neat, though.
- Every piece of gear you will ever own will be a compromise between what you need and what you can afford.
- A full 30% of your best photographs will be lucky accidents.
- The Zone System of exposure control doesn't work, but it's better than random guessing.
- "It's better to photograph with the camera you own than to wait for the camera you want." Adapted from *Stephen Stills*
- "The photographers with the most good photographs are the ones who spend the most time photographing." *Stewart Harvey*
- Photographic technique is easy to master, but lack of it is an incredibly handy excuse for poor work.

- The hardest thing to do in photography, as in life, is to make a commitment.
- The production of a "greatest hit" is always the result of immersing oneself thoroughly in a project. To set out to make a "greatest hit" photograph will always fail.
- If you're looking for a social art, try dancing.
- The more a photographic chemical smells, costs, or degrades with time or heat, the better it is supposed to be. This is simply not true. Great photographs are not the result of exotic chemicals – they result from the application of a creative mind.
- At least nine times out of ten, there is a conflict between marketing potential and artistic value.
- The worst technical problem of all is an unknown hair stuck inside the camera at the film plane.
- It is much harder to make a good black and white photograph than a color one.
- Even after the most careful and meticulous metering and exposure calculations, it is still a good idea to bracket.
- It is impossible to make a good photograph with uranium salt toning, Kodalith, or RC paper.
- If someone made a $40 cable release, I'd buy one. No, I'd buy two – one for a back-up.
- Whoever first makes an affordable, lightweight, sturdy, durable, and functional tripod will retire very rich.
- Taking meticulous field notes is a waste of time unless you are fully committed to reviewing them later.
- The time spent organizing negatives and digital files is worth it.
- There is no magic developing formula. Any developer will work fine providing you thoroughly learn how to use it.
- The debate between enlarger cold light heads and condenser heads is a total waste of time. The debate between analog and digital media is a total waste of time. To think that one specific kind of equipment makes better photographs misses the point. Better photographers make better photographs. Equipment is never the answer to producing great work.

- A well-tested and intelligently employed used lens is better than an untested, new and expensive one.
- Faith is good. Knowledge is good. To confuse the two is foolish.
- There is no such thing as a "perfect exposure." If you have to error on one side or the other, more exposure is always better than less. With slides and digital cameras, read this sentence backwards.
- Manufacturer's film speed ratings are meaningless and quite often laughable.
- Bigger prints are not always better, but better prints are always better.
- It is not the size of the print that counts, but the "size" of the impact it makes on the viewer's brain/heart that matters.
- To give away 10 prints is more rewarding than to sell one. But, to sell ten prints is more rewarding than to give away one!
- The more gear you carry, the less likely you are to make a good photograph.
- The most influential technical decision is not which film, camera, lens or exposure setting to use, but whether or not to use a tripod.
- No amount of darkroom/Photoshop work can make up for a badly exposed or composed image.
- The most valuable personality traits for photographers are patience and humor. The most troublesome are perfectionism and procrastination.
- Without compassion, photography is a bore.
- Critics are valuable to Art – and you should ignore them while making photographs.
- Photography classes can be of some help. Workshops are better. The instructor makes or breaks either.
- Workshops and/or instructors can be addictive and can take up valuable time better spent doing photography.
- It is better to study with an instructor who wants to help you develop your own work, even if it is very different from theirs,

than to study with one who wants to tell you how they did their work.

- If your main interest in a workshop is to learn how the photographer "did it," so you can "do it" too, question your motives.
- A good photograph is never "about light." Good photographs are about feelings.
- A good photograph, when first seen, hits you like a ton of bricks. A better photograph is often unseen at first, but comes back to mind over and over again long after you've stopped looking at it. This often happens unexpectedly.
- Lots of photographers will claim that a photograph that needs a caption is an inferior photograph. This is silly and denies the obvious fact that all photographs are made, seen and interpreted against a social background that influences their appreciation and understanding.
- Creating art requires money.
- "Every artist has a responsibility to their art that includes the creative creation of a stable, personal financial base." *David Grant Best*
- The most expensive part of photography is not the cameras, the film, the paper or the chemistry. It is the travel.
- For 99.999% of all negatives, there is no functional difference between limiting it to 50 prints and limiting it to five prints. You will never make print #3.
- If you price your work over $20, you have eliminated 99% of the people in the world from your potential market.
- "Artists who take up photography, find their 'photographic turf' more quickly than photographers who decide to make Art." *Stewart Harvey*
- "Good photographic composition is merely the strongest way of seeing." *Edward Weston*
- Every photographer has dry spells. Good photographers work anyway. Those who do grow by leaps and bounds.
- Most photographers who claim they cannot sell their work have very little inventory on hand. Selling is, to a large degree,

proportional to the number of choices you can offer a potential buyer.

- Another photographer, when seeing your work, will often try to help by offering comments about how they would have done it. This is the epitome of insensitivity.
- "Any photographer worth his salt has 10,000 bad negatives under his belt." *Ansel Adams*
- The process of photography is more important than the product.
- "The word *photographer* is a verb." *Ted Orland*
- When a photographer can deeply appreciate another's work and not feel compelled to duplicate it, they have begun to mature.
- Show 25 photographs to 25 people and you'll find there are at least 15 different choices of a favorite.
- If you find, while reviewing a proof sheet, that you do not remember taking a particular photograph, print that one first. It will be the best photograph on the roll.
- Extra batteries will, eventually, save the day.
- The most valuable asset you can take with you into the field is an extra day.
- Drugstores in small towns never stock sheet film. Curiously enough, they do stock digital memory cards.
- Someone once said, "If you can't make a great photograph of a mundane subject, make a mundane photograph of a great subject." If these are your only two choices, take up knitting.
- Developing a new gimmick genre of photography may get you some press, but it also will get you forgotten.
- The tortoise does, in fact, beat the hare.
- Galleries, like banks, are more than happy to help you providing you can demonstrate that you don't need it.
- Very few photographs would not be improved by being printed somewhat lighter.
- D-max never is. Archival is a relative term. The "circle of confusion" is aptly named.
- Acquiring a new camera can be both a door and an excuse.

- Infrared film is a fun and useless phase. There are a few exceptions, but even the great photographers went through the phase, too.
- Very few people can cut a square mat. Even fewer can cut a square window. Good oval mats are a direct gift from God.
- "Most famous photographers work their entire life and produce tens of thousands of negatives and hundreds or perhaps thousands of prints but are remembered for less than ten and famous for just one." *Cherie Hiser*
- "The fault with most photographers is that they spend 1/60th of a second making a photograph and the rest of their life explaining it." *Richard Brown*
- We are fast approaching critical mass on photographs of nudes on a sand dune, sand dunes with no nudes, Yosemite, weathered barns, the church at Taos, New Mexico, lacy waterfalls, fields of cut hay in the afternoon sun, abandoned houses, crashing waves, sunsets in color, and reflected peaks in a mountain lake.
- Always eat before going to a gallery opening and avoid, at all costs, anything with shrimp in it. Trust me on this one.
- Never ask a person who collects cameras if you can see his photographs.
- Purging your negative files in a giant bonfire is both scary and a relief.
- What you photograph says as much about an internal and personal process as it does about an external bit of subject matter.
- The quality of a photograph is inversely proportional to the amount of intellect used and directly proportional to the amount of intuition used when composing it.
- "If a photographer really expects to produce great work, they must, just like musicians, be prepared to practice their craft *every* day. This does not mean you must take pictures every day, but you must at least practice *seeing* every day." *David Bayles*

- The more controversial your work is, the more press you will receive and the more people will talk about you and your art. This means nothing, but it will open doors that were previously closed.
- If you create controversial art just so it will open doors, you will be disappointed at the fleeting nature of fame.
- The most amazing thing about Weston's *Pepper #30* is not that he made a great photograph of a pepper, but that he saw it as photographic subject material. The second most amazing thing is that he endured 29 "failures" to make the one that satisfied him. Few people remember his *Banana #18*, but he made it.
- A large negative records more detail than a smaller one.
- Just as a large negative records more detail than a smaller one, a large mind is more emotionally sensitive than a small mind.
- More pixels do not mean more detail.
- If your budget is limited, buy a cheap camera and the best lens you can afford.
- Making a photograph is a cumulative process with each step accumulating degradation.
- If your work looks like someone else's, ask yourself why and don't answer right away. Think about this deeply. If you do, your work will become better almost immediately.
- Don't be shy about approaching "famous" photographers. They are, almost without exception, giving and generous people who will be happy to help you if you are serious about learning.
- Before you sink a lot of time and money into your MFA degree, think carefully about what you will do after you graduate.
- If your work gains attention because of your extraordinary craft and technique, your fame will be fleeting. Pretty soon, everyone will be able to easily do work that is just as good as your masterpiece of craftsmanship from today. When that happens, your work will have to stand on the merit of its artistic content alone. The role of the artist is clearest when everyone can do it.

- "It is easy to make a picture of someone and call it a portrait. The difficulty lies in making a picture that makes the viewer care about a stranger." *Paul Strand*
- There is art. There is entertainment. They are not the same thing, but when a piece of work is both, it achieves a higher plateau.
- It is easier to make a viewer angry than it is to make them cry. It is most difficult to make them laugh.
- Organizing and planning is good as long as you don't use it as a clever procrastination device to avoid doing the real work.
- Don't allow yourself to become too enamored with your current choices of equipment and techniques. There will be new stuff that will make everything you now do and use obsolete.
- Although everything you learn will become obsolete, it will be your foundation. As long as you are working, there is no truly "wasted" time.
- Permanently dry-mounting your work to a mat board virtually guarantees that mat board will become dirty and dinged. You will be better served to mat your work so it can be removed at a later time and matted again, if necessary. You will learn this when "the big gallery" calls you for a career-making show – next month. Take this advice seriously.
- Finishing work which you later think is bad is far better than waiting until you can finish it better. The only way to get to better is by working through the bad.
- In ten years, most of your work today will seem trivial and dated. A small percentage won't. This is why you photograph.
- You would never know it by looking at the photographic press, but there are an amazing number of creative people engaged in photography who couldn't care less about equipment, but who love photographs.
- "Learning" and "living" are two words for the same process.
- It makes absolutely no difference whatsoever to the audience what your process is, your trials and tribulations, your

methods, your equipment, your pain and suffering. All of this is irrelevant to the image – and this information should remain unknown and unpublished.

- Materials are more fleeting than light. Light is a constant that will remain part of the photographic process throughout the ages. Materials have a life span of a dozen years or so. Get used to the idea that your favorite photograph-producing materials will be discontinued in your lifetime.

- Photographs, even as artifacts, are not unique nor are they precious. Human emotions expressed in art are the valuable commodity that raises artwork to something special.

- All artwork is seen and understood in the context of society. As time goes on, the symbols that make your artwork understandable will, in the future, make your artwork incomprehensible.

- Never forget that your photographs are a slice of time. If time, movement, moment, or the passage or stillness of time is not a part of your photograph, then you are missing one of the most important components of a photograph.

- There is nothing more boring in a portfolio of images than the repetition of bullet composition – every subject in the dead center of the image.

- Abstracts are one of the most interesting forms of photography, but you can't give them away.

- Whenever there is an advance in technology (e.g., silver versus platinum, or digital versus analog) there will be a debate and argument of ferocious proportions as to which is the true medium. All such discussions are a diversion from the path of creativity and any time spent in the debate is lost to the process of making your art.

- Technology that allows you to make images faster and with more instantaneous feedback may be both better and worse than slower, more cumbersome technologies. Value judgments about technology are only meaningful in the context of how the technologies are used.

- Although stability and weight are important components of

tripods, the most important characteristic is its vertical range – both higher and lower than your normal standing line of sight. This is also the most underused characteristic of tripods.

- There is no tripod that can withstand even a 30-mile per hour wind. To make tack-sharp images requires a windless day or at least a windless moment during the exposure.

- Kodak recommends that you place the sun over your shoulder for the best pictures. Their advice is exactly backwards.

- When photographing in the landscape, always carry a can of Fix-A-Flat. No, carry two cans.

- The most useful filter of all is a brown one.

- Always manage the edges – in your prints, in your driving, in your tripod placements, in your choice of subjects, and in life in general. Wherever there is an edge there is power, tension, and the potential for failure.

- Cloudless skies are difficult. Gray skies are difficult. In between these extremes is the sweet spot. The same could be said for sunny days and sunless days, no filters and too much filtration, no dodging or burning and too much dodging or burning, no toning or too much toning. Abandon moderation only with extreme care.

- Most photographs have an aspect ratio that is determined by the aspect ratio of the film. The aspect ratio of your prints should, instead, be determined by the composition and the subject.

- Like *haiku*, landscape photographs should always have a visual reference to either the weather or the season.

- It is impossible to make a photograph of a cat that is not trite. For some unknown reason, this does not apply to dogs.

- Great ideas rarely bonk you on the head like a falling asteroid. Instead, they gently tap you on the shoulder like a falling feather.

- If there are three ways to do something, the best way to do it will probably be the fourth way you think of.

- Edge-trimming prints perfectly rectilinear is almost

impossible to do with precision. It is much easier to use a perfectly rectilinear easel or a perfect computerized crop.

- Making photographs, like viewing photographs, is best as an emotional and intuitive process. The challenge is that producing photographs is mostly an intellectual, mechanical, and technical process. Knowing when, where, and how to draw the line between these two is as important a skill as anything you could learn about photography.
- Politics makes for great sport and bad art.
- When you are absolutely stuck and can't think of anything to photograph, photograph anything as a means to develop momentum again.
- Applying diffusion or an irregular border will not make a bad image more interesting. It will make it more gimmicky.
- Some things are just more photogenic than others: shiny steel is more photogenic than rusty metal, anger is more photogenic than passivity.
- Photograph and engage life as though it is very short. It is – as you will learn when you see how quickly the next ten years go by.
- And lastly, in the cosmic scale of things, photography is not that important.